THE BEDFORD SERIES IN HISTORY AND CULTURE

Attitudes toward Sex
in Antebellum America

A Brief History with Documents

THE BEDFORD SERIES IN HISTORY AND CULTURE

Attitudes toward Sex in Antebellum America

A Brief History with Documents

Helen Lefkowitz Horowitz

Smith College

BEDFORD/ST. MARTIN'S   Boston ◆ New York

To my Smith College students, present and past.

For Bedford/St. Martin's

Executive Editor for History: Mary V. Dougherty
Director of Development for History: Jane Knetzger
Developmental Editor: Shannon Hunt
Senior Production Supervisor: Dennis Conroy
Senior Marketing Manager: Jenna Bookin Barry
Project Management: Books By Design, Inc.
Indexer: Books By Design, Inc.
Text Design: Claire Seng-Niemoeller
Cover Design: Billy Boardman
Cover Art: Lola Has Come! Lithograph, 1852. Collection of Helen Lefkowitz Horowitz.
Composition: Stratford Publishing Services, Inc.
Printing and Binding: Haddon Craftsmen, an RR Donnelley & Sons Company

President: Joan E. Feinberg
Editorial Director: Denise B. Wydra
Director of Marketing: Karen Melton Soeltz
Director of Editing, Design, and Production: Marcia Cohen
Manager, Publishing Services: Emily Berleth

Library of Congress Control Number: 2005931064

Manufactured in the United States of America.

8   7   6   5   4
l   k   j   i   h

For information, write: Bedford/St. Martin's, 75 Arlington Street, Boston, MA 02116
(617-399-4000)

ISBN-10: 0-312-41226-6 (paperback)
          1-4039-7155-2 (hardcover)
ISBN-13: 978-0-312-41226-5 (paperback)
          978-1-4039-7155-5 (hardcover)

Foreword

The Bedford Series in History and Culture is designed so that readers can study the past as historians do.

The historian's first task is finding the evidence. Documents, letters, memoirs, interviews, pictures, movies, novels, or poems can provide facts and clues. Then the historian questions and compares the sources. There is more to do than in a courtroom, for hearsay evidence is welcome, and the historian is usually looking for answers beyond act and motive. Different views of an event may be as important as a single verdict. How a story is told may yield as much information as what it says.

Along the way the historian seeks help from other historians and perhaps from specialists in other disciplines. Finally, it is time to write, to decide on an interpretation and how to arrange the evidence for readers.

Each book in this series contains an important historical document or group of documents, each document a witness from the past and open to interpretation in different ways. The documents are combined with some element of historical narrative—an introduction or a biographical essay, for example—that provides students with an analysis of the primary source material and important background information about the world in which it was produced.

Each book in the series focuses on a specific topic within a specific historical period. Each provides a basis for lively thought and discussion about several aspects of the topic and the historian's role. Each is short enough (and inexpensive enough) to be a reasonable one-week assignment in a college course. Whether as classroom or personal reading, each book in the series provides firsthand experience of the challenge—and fun—of discovering, recreating, and interpreting the past.

Lynn Hunt
David W. Blight
Bonnie G. Smith
Natalie Zemon Davis
Ernest R. May

Preface

Attitudes toward Sex in Antebellum America is a documentary history that offers a fresh approach to the history of sexuality, presenting a much richer portrait of nineteenth-century sexual understanding and viewpoints than is conventionally available to students and instructors. The nineteenth century has long been viewed as "Victorian," or repressed. In actuality, the antebellum era witnessed a vital public discussion of sexuality—much of which was forced underground only in the years after the 1873 Comstock Law, a federal statute that criminalized obscene words and images, contraceptive information, and abortion advertisements. As a result of the Comstock Law, many publications containing sexual content were suppressed or destroyed. This book brings back to light those primary sources written by and for the group for whom society was very much in flux during the antebellum era—white, middle-class Northeasterners whose lives were profoundly changed by the Industrial Revolution. This collection of documents demonstrates that these antebellum men and, in particular, women were actively engaged in commentary and controversy about sex, sexuality, reproduction, and their own bodies and desires. Their words resonate today, as twenty-first-century Americans discuss and debate many of the same issues and concerns.

Americans' deliberations about sex in the decades before the Civil War can be grouped into four areas or frameworks: folk wisdom, evangelical religion, popular science, and sexual radicalism. It is useful to imagine these frameworks as four voices in a conversation, each expressing a different point of view. Folk wisdom, or vernacular sexuality, the first framework, held an earthy acceptance of sex and desire as an essential aspect of life. By contrast, the evangelical Christianity fostered by the Second Great Awakening held a deep distrust of the appetites and passions of the body. By the 1830s, reform physiology, a new and important popular science of the body, came into being. This third perspective brought together scientific notions of the body, health, nerves, and the relation of body and mind. Finally, in the decade before the Civil War, a fourth framework of sexual radicalism emerged, putting sex at the center of life.

When thought of as voices engaged in public deliberation, these frameworks allow us to understand antebellum sexual attitudes in a fluid and complex way. By contrast, common notions of Victorian sexuality set up a single dynamic of repression and release, presumably set in motion by self-control, suppression of sexual urges, and denial of women's sexuality. Shifting to the four frameworks, we can see the partial truth of this, that evangelical Christian ministers and some of the representative writers of reform physiology did argue for sexual restraint. But the documents collected here allow us to understand that these voices were part of a larger public discussion of sexuality that ranged from advocates of sexual restriction to those of sexual enthusiasm and considered many other important topics, such as contraception, abortion, masturbation, prostitution, and the commercial production of racy materials.

In attempting to re-create the complex public conversation about sex in the antebellum era, this book demonstrates its many links to issues of the period. In the introduction, I place the documents in their broad historical context, suggesting what they mean and how they transform our understanding of sexuality in the decades before the Civil War. Particularly in the North, the Industrial Revolution's many changes reshaped the contours of American lives in the antebellum years. In the same era that women experienced the pulls of law and ideology that drew them more tightly into the domestic arena, new work opportunities outside the home enabled their movement into the public realm. Married couples sought to limit the number of their children. As more and more people moved into the middle class, new issues and new fears shaped their understanding of the human body. A growing commercial world in emerging cities offered both opportunities and dangers, and fresh intellectual, scientific, religious, and literary influences came into play. Discussion of sex was never separate from the cultural and social life of women and men, but rather was a vital part of it. Moreover, sexual discussion mattered not only in helping to shape private behavior, but also in informing public choices about masturbation, contraception, abortion, homosexuality, prostitution, and printed matter.

The first group of documents features voices from each of the four frameworks, showing how new issues and voices came into play over time. The second set of documents presents materials from the world

of commerce. Changes in printing and marketing brought new opportunities for sexualized words and images in newspapers and books.
In American cities, prostitution flourished, as did writing about it.
The line between advice and commerce became blurred in advertisements for birth control and abortion services. Sporting men, defiant
of middle-class respectability, took their pleasures in establishments
aimed at capturing their business, such as saloons, brothels, and theaters, and the sporting press documented and encouraged the pursuit
of their interests. Lastly, the coda presents the federal Comstock Law
of 1873 that ushered public deliberation about sex into a new and
more limited era.

This volume features a number of pedagogical aids to guide and
inform readers as they approach the documents. Each selection is pre-
ceded by a headnote that extends the context and interpretation
offered in the introduction. Footnotes define or explain obscure words
or references. Illustrations offer a glimpse into the visual world of
antebellum print as it dealt with sexual matters. The chronology following the documents helps students place the readings within their
specific time period and in relation to political and public events. I
have taught these materials to my own students, and their inquiries as
well as my own shaped the questions for consideration. The bibliogra-
phy encourages readers to probe more deeply into the secondary literature around the sources. Finally, the index serves as a guide to
specific topics, authors, and themes. All in all, the intention of this
book is both to present fascinating and informative documents that
allow a new understanding of antebellum life and to make this material teachable in ways that engage students in important issues.

A NOTE ABOUT THE COVER

In the 1840s, a dancer taking the name "Lola Montez" created great
excitement in the press when she arrived on the American stage. Lola
Montez was one of the first celebrities in American popular culture. At
the time of the image, she was especially known for her "spider
dance," during which she shook off imaginary spiders in a way considered sexually suggestive. On the cover, she is depicted in a short
skirt before a manager, nonchalantly putting on his glove, and an audience of two. Seated in front of her is a somber man, who holds a paper
entitled "Sober Thoughts" as he peeks at the dancer through his hand
over his face. In a box, a gentleman holds the *New York Herald,* then

regarded as a sensational newspaper. This image, along with a companion, "Lola Coming!" appeared in *The Old Soldier,* a New York periodical (Vol. 1, No. 1, January 1, 1852) and was most likely the work of
lithographer John L. Magee.

ACKNOWLEDGMENTS

In working on this book, I have had a great deal of help. Dan
Horowitz, Sarah Horowitz, colleagues, and friends helped me think
through the issues and write the monograph *Rereading Sex,* which
guided me as I chose documents and wrote the introduction and head-
notes for this book. I tried out a draft in an American studies course at
Smith College. Students in the class contributed significantly to revision by their excellent discussion of the documents, questions, and
suggestions for change. I was fortunate in the research assistance of
students Rebecca D'Orsagna, Umayyah Cable, and Sarah Kanabay,
now Smith alumnae. I am grateful to Smith College for funds for
research. I was also fortunate in the excellent readers of the manu-
script whose careful critiques guided revision: Timothy J. Gilfoyle,
Loyola University of Chicago; Amy Greenberg, Pennsylvania State
University; Judith Giesberg, Villanova University; Jacqueline Camp-
bell, University of Connecticut; Gail Bederman, University of Notre
Dame; and Judith Houck, University of Wisconsin–Madison. At Bed-
ford/St. Martin's, I have had the excellent encouragement and professional aid of editors Jane Knetzger and Shannon Hunt and production
manager Emily Berleth.

Helen Lefkowitz Horowitz

Contents

APPENDIXES

Illustrations

THE BEDFORD SERIES IN HISTORY AND CULTURE

Attitudes toward Sex
in Antebellum America

A Brief History with Documents

PART ONE

Introduction: Voices in the Sexual Conversation in Antebellum America

"Attitudes toward Sex in Antebellum America" must seem to some readers a ridiculous subject. Wasn't prudery in that era so extreme that piano legs were covered by pantaloons? A typical reaction to this topic by students and colleagues has been to ask with a laugh, "What? Was there more than one?"

It is the hope of this book to convince you that, indeed, there were diverse attitudes, and that you will share in the enthusiasm for their discovery.

Undeniably, sex is an amusing subject, but it is also one of critical importance to society. The ability to discuss sexual matters in the public arena is one of the great historical changes reshaping the lives of American women and men. Its impact on human life in the antebellum era is comparable to the rise of democratic fervor, industrialization, education, and the emergence of popular culture.[1] As this book focuses more on ideas than behavior, it draws on public writing rather than personal correspondence. The documents in Part Two enable students to examine the manifold ways in which sexual matters were written about and discussed in the public arena.

So, how did Americans imagine sex in the nineteenth century? How did they understand desire? The answers to these questions diverge significantly from the conventional story of nineteenth-century sexual repression, typically called "Victorian." The reason for this discrepancy between the evidence and popular belief was that censorship distorted the historical record. Especially after 1873, when the Comstock

Law banned the mailing of sexually explicit material, agents of the law confiscated and destroyed books, pamphlets, and periodicals they deemed obscene (see Document 33). Thus materials crucial to the understanding of antebellum sexual attitudes are absent from rare book collections and archives. A historian of sexuality, therefore, has to be a detective, seeking and uncovering historical matter deliberately destroyed or hidden.

The documents recovered from this period tell a complicated story with no single narrative line. Antebellum Americans disagreed about many matters—economic, religious, and ideological—and sexuality was no exception. Cultural divides created several distinct understandings of the body, reproduction, and desire. Four stances, or "frameworks"—vernacular sexuality, evangelical Christianity, popular science, and sexual radicalism—shaped the ways Americans conveyed and received sexual knowledge in print. Earthy folk understandings acknowledged sex and desire as vital aspects of life for men and women. By contrast, evangelical Christianity held a deep distrust of the flesh. (Its position has dominated historical memory.) Beginning in 1831, a new and important popular science of the body emerged, called reform physiology in its day. This third perspective brought together scientific notions of the body, nerves, health, and the relationship between mind and body. By the 1850s, a fourth framework emerged at the radical edge of reform physiology, placing sex at the center of life.

Antebellum Americans who read and reflected on the new literature about sex were part—and only a part—of a robust society in the midst of great change. Americans living in the Northeast were among those who experienced the most profound transformation of daily life. There, industrialization drew women and men into factories. Commerce offered new opportunities for migrants from farms and immigrants from abroad, and cities grew rapidly. Reading increased as town common schools, supported by taxes, encouraged all white children, girls and boys, to attend.

Writers and readers of the following documents, therefore, were located primarily in the more settled and literate Northeast. Also, those writers and readers were (or were presumed to be) white. Northern states gradually ended slavery, with the last Northern slave freed in New York in 1827; but the quarter-of-a-million free African Americans, north and south, whether a tiny minority or a sizable proportion of a locality's population, were typically treated as inferiors and suffered deep discrimination. In the South, meanwhile, the institution of slavery grew rapidly with the spread of cotton culture and settlement to the lower south and southwest. Because the sexual culture of the South must include slavery, it requires a separate inquiry into issues that cannot be treated adequately in this book.

Although most white women in the antebellum era continued to live their lives primarily within the family circle, many had been profoundly affected by the American Revolution, which drew them into the public realm and required some to head their households during the war. In the period of constitution building, however, free women found that rights that had once protected them in inheritance and property were now taken away. The new states accepted the 1765–69 codification of English common law that turned married women into legal nonentities. Common law's notion of *couverture* declared that a woman's legal identity was "covered" by that of her husband. Once the Jacksonian era opened suffrage to all adult white males, white women's inability to vote was solely because of their sex.

Not only were all women barred from voting, they could not be elected to office, serve on juries, or be lawyers or judges. They were also denied the opportunities afforded men for higher education. Thus they could not receive training for the learned professions, such as law, medicine, or the ministry, except irregularly, and access to these vocations was typically blocked. They were excluded from apprenticeships that allowed entry into the crafts, and even irregular training was normally impeded by prejudice, assumptions about women's appropriate sphere, and fear of economic competition. Women who went into fields such as printing generally followed their husbands' crafts as wives and widows. As a rule, women did not speak in public to mixed audiences.

The American Revolution left white women a key legacy, however. In its wake, white women were perceived as Republican Mothers, responsible for the education of republican sons. Rhetoric placed a new value on the home as the Nursery of the Republic. As the middle class came into being, the home attained new importance. Although America had always known "middling folk," those who were neither rich nor poor, commercial and industrial developments increased their numbers and altered their consciousness. Emerging business houses and factories required a large number of literate persons to keep the organizations running. Growing cities offered livelihood to lawyers, doctors, writers, architects, and engineers. A literature arose to guide women into this newly conscious middle class. Much has been made of the significance of this writing for morality: It emphasized the home as a moral center and gave rules for establishing order and restraint. A central element, however, was instruction that incorporated household work into modern life through planning and organization.

Domestic changes came at a time of economic transformation that separated male labor from the house. As a result, female status became equated with seclusion within its four walls. White women who remained at home were told they were different from and better than the slaves or lower-class women who labored for them or who otherwise worked outside their own dwellings. Preachers and writers offered the rhetorical "cult of true womanhood" to sequestered women, assuring them that they were purer and more spiritual than men.

Yet other changes were simultaneously working to draw women's interests outside the home. The broadening market brought them onto the streets to acquire goods. Girls as well as boys attended the common school. As women increasingly became readers, they constituted a new audience for public prints and a new market for reading. Academies and seminaries rose up across the settled regions to educate females as teachers and mothers. Teaching offered the first clearly middle-class occupation to women, allowing them to earn money and live apart from their families. In addition, the early mills drew on the labor of farm daughters. Coming into towns such as Lowell, teenage girls earned relatively high wages as they labored in factories and lived in boarding houses. Working in schools and factories and running households, many American women entered into a world run by clock time and organized by system. Finally, reform movements drew middle-class women into association. Gathering first in churches, they focused on family, temperance, and abolition. Pioneer women's rights advocates argued for legal and property rights, increased opportunities for education and employment, and, beginning with the first women's rights convention in 1848, suffrage.

Theater offered women special opportunities and risks. In the antebellum years, prominent actresses, typically immigrants from England, stepped onstage in American cities to take key dramatic roles, entering the public sphere to expand conventional notions of womanhood. In an era that saw the beginnings of celebrity, however, their public lives and stage presence under the male gaze made them vulnerable to sexual objectification onstage and association with sexual immorality off. Female actors experienced in an extreme form issues that other women encountered as they moved into the public arena. Prostitution was a big and thriving business in American cities. The relatively high monetary returns of brothel life attracted young females who were barred from most other forms of remunerative employment. In turn, the old association of "women of the streets" or "public women" with prostitution heightened the vulnerability of all women, including female lecturers, shopkeepers, clerks, milliners, and chambermaids, as they went about their occupations in the city.

VOICES IN THE PUBLIC DELIBERATION OF SEX: THE FOUR FRAMEWORKS

Public deliberation of sex flourished within this changing world. By the 1830s, three of the four frameworks for understanding sexuality were already in play, and, by the 1850s, they were joined by the fourth. All of them were spoken as well as written, but the available record involves only print, although this includes lectures transcribed at the time and later published. The expression that best conveys antebellum sexuality is a conversation. Readers should try and imagine Americans in the era before the Civil War as engaged in a complex three- or four-way conversation about sex. In the exchange, each side not merely disagreed; each imagined sexuality from a distinct cultural perspective. Each of the four stances shaped the way Americans received and conveyed sexual knowledge.[2]

The notion of a conversation allows both the richness of the interplay between ideas in an era and the possibility of disconnection and internal conflict. One can imagine an individual person from the past receiving contending messages and absorbing them variously into life and practice. Ideas about sex matter, but their relation to sexual practice is complex and even mysterious.

Vernacular Sexual Culture

The first framework—folk wisdom—was part of vernacular culture, the mentality of ordinary people. The use of the term *vernacular* signifies that it lay outside the literate discourses of religion, science, and law and was typically despised by those in power. Although vernacular culture was largely an oral tradition, passed down through the generations and sideways among peers, elements appeared in print in *Aristotle's Master-piece* (see Document 1), a venerable compendium of sexual matters.

Using the name of the ancient Greek philosopher Aristotle largely to give the work authority (see Figure 1), the anonymous authors drew on an eclectic mix of medical lore, including classical sources, seventeenth-century treatises, and popular folklore. The book was first published in English in 1684, and, within a year, eight copies, presumably printed in England, appeared in a Boston bookseller's inventory. By the mid-eighteenth century, *Aristotle's Master-piece* was widely available beyond the cultural centers of seaport cities such as Boston, in such provincial outposts as Northampton, Massachusetts, one hundred miles to the west. Rooted in the ancient past, contested first by Christian tradition and then in the eighteenth century by rational approaches, *Aristotle's Master-piece* was reprinted in many editions and remained a source of popular wisdom throughout the nineteenth century.

At the time the book was compiled, scientists, medical men, and common people shared similar ideas regarding the human body. Harking back to ancient Greece, the work envisioned the body as comprised of solids—such as blood vessels and nerves—and fluids. Physical and mental health and well-being came with the equilibrium of four bodily fluids called humors, related to the four states—hot, cold, dry, and moist—and the four prime elements—fire, air, earth, and water. Although some of its readers were women, *Aristotle's Master-piece* presented a largely male perspective and slighted women's vernacular sexual culture, which centered on childbirth and efforts to control fertility rather than on sexual intercourse. Nevertheless, the book demonstrates to readers that seventeenth-century women and their doctors knew about medications to induce abortion, something confirmed by recent historical research.[3]

Vernacular sexuality in America was the source of bawdy humor, many popular terms, and, as literacy spread, numerous sexually arousing texts comprising much of the lively commerce in erotic printed materials. Lying at the base of conscious awareness and corresponding to strong bodily urges, folk wisdom retained power throughout the nineteenth century. Although plenty of prescriptive statements from the pulpit or the printed page shaped what Americans thought and felt, they did not fully supplant what many saw as common knowledge.

Evangelical Christianity

Christian ministers were certainly aware of vernacular sexuality, as for them it was a central component of man's wickedness. Men such as Lyman Beecher (see Documents 2 and 3) described God's fallen angel

Figure 1. *Frontispiece,* Aristotle's Compleat Master-piece, *1741.* The great philosopher Aristotle receives into his writing chamber a woman covered with furry tufts and a small black child, two of the many medical "problems" that the accompanying text attempted to explain.

Boston Medical Library in the Francis A. Countway Library of Medicine.

7

Satan warring against the Gospel. Ever since God placed "Old Man Adam" on earth, Satan had enticed him to sin. And "Eve," that representative wayward woman, was no help. In their pulpits, ministers such as Beecher thundered against the temptations of the devil. As a result, lust became an important deadly sin in the nineteenth century. Flaming sexual passion put men in peril of the Hell to come. Such evangelical Christian beliefs constituted the second framework for the public deliberation of sex.

Beecher was nurtured both in the Western philosophical tradition with its basis in Greek and Roman thought and in Christianity as modified by Puritans, the dominant Protestant group settling in New England. This heritage presents complexities to those attempting to understand sexual desire and its expression. At least since Roman times, the church saw sex as suspect. Carnal urges came from the depraved animal nature of men and women linked to the Fall. The Catholic church fathers stated that although it is better to marry than to burn in Hell, it is better not to marry. Virginity was the ideal. However, over time the Church moved from denial of the flesh to an acceptance of sexual expression in marriage. Beginning in the mid-sixteenth century, Catholic writers instructed priests in the confessional to distinguish between sexual acts that were "natural," leading to procreation, and those regarded as "unnatural," such as masturbation and sodomy. Ordinary men and women were taught to examine not only what they did but how they felt, and sin was extended to unnatural sexual desire and the play of the imagination.

Protestants amended this message to stress its counters: It is not good for humans to live alone; people should be fruitful and multiply. The Puritans who came to America accepted and validated sexual intercourse. Grounding their theology in the science of their day, Puritan ministers insisted on the duty and pleasure of sexual union in marriage. Yet like other Protestants, Puritans worried about sexual excess. During the eighteenth century, Protestantism splintered into denominations, some moving toward rationalism, some emphasizing spiritual rebirth and revival. In a few elite circles, emphasis on the natural and material world opened the way to opposition to organized religion and allowed some to experiment with the sexual license associated with the French aristocracy. The Second Great Awakening, a religious revival that began in the 1790s and reached a crescendo in the 1820s and 1830s, brought back older Christian notions about human nature and sin. Revivalists joined in a war against many sins of the flesh, including lust. The Second Great Awakening fostered reform movements that called on Christians to reorder society and culture in ways to keep human passions in control.

Reform Physiology

By the 1820s, evangelical Christians found themselves in conflict with freethinkers, who were encouraging more scientific approaches to sexuality. In the 1830s, the freethinkers were joined by Christian reformers who attempted to blend science and religious practice. Together they developed the third framework, a popular science of the body, known in its era as reform physiology.

FREETHINKING

In the late 1820s, Frances Wright, Robert Dale Owen, and other freethinkers demanded a new approach to sexual questions. They valued frank, open discussion of sexual matters. Collectively, freethinkers initiated a new voice in public deliberation about sex.

Both Wright and Owen immigrated to America, bringing with them hopes for radical change. In 1825, Robert Dale Owen (see Figure 2), the son of British industrialist and philanthropist Robert Owen, came to New Harmony, Indiana, to oversee his father's utopian effort in the United States. Frances Wright (see Figure 3), a Scottish heiress and writer, settled in America in 1825 with the idea of founding her own utopian community. When this scheme failed, she went on the lecture circuit and, in 1829, moved to New York. There she established the Hall of Science, a lecture hall and bookstore, and, with Owen, now in New York, published the weekly newspaper the *Free Enquirer.* These enterprises introduced many ideas of the Enlightenment into American discussions of sex.

The philosophic movement in Europe and America known as the Enlightenment emphasized the power of reason and the orderliness of a universe shaped by natural law. Because it encouraged the search for natural causes of phenomena, Enlightenment thinking was an important stimulus to science and medicine. As Americans studied abroad, they brought home methods and theories of Scottish and French medical practice, including new understandings of the brain and the nervous system. These held that the human brain was the seat of consciousness. The nerves—often perceived as tiny hollow tubes emanating from the brain—traveled to all parts of the body and were responsible for perception and knowledge. The brain controlled the passions, sending impressions to bodily organs, including the sexual

Figure 2.   *Robert Dale Owen, Sketch from Life, ca. 1830.*   An important free-thinker, Owen came to the United States in 1825 to run the utopian community founded by his father. Published in 1831, his *Moral Physiology* encouraged and offered advice on contraceptive use. He later had an important political career in Indiana and served in the U.S. House of Representatives.

From *Robert Dale Owen: A Biography* by Richard William Leopold (Cambridge, Mass.: Harvard University Press, 1940).

ones, and could be healthy or diseased. By the late eighteenth century, the brain was also seen as the location of the imagination. Such notions underlay the new discipline of psychology, which was beginning to emerge out of philosophy. These new theories about the brain and nerves had a powerful impact on the understanding of human sexuality.

Figure 3. *Frances Wright, Painting by Henry Inman, ca. 1824.* The year this portrait was painted, Wright accompanied the Revolutionary War hero the Marquis de Lafayette on a trip to the United States. A year later she returned to begin her career as an important freethinker, utopian, lecturer, writer, and advocate of new approaches to sexual questions. Her controversial ideas on women and race later provoked derogatory depictions of her that contrast sharply with this feminine representation.

Frances Wright, 1824 (oil on canvas), Inman, Henry (1801–46)/© Collection of the New-York Historical Society, USA/The Bridgeman Art Library.

Elements of the older traditions persisted, however. The Enlightenment emphasized the roles of reason and control over instinct and passion. Medical practice largely left the female body and its reproductive organs to midwifery. Although the new empirical science based on observation and experiment made great inroads on understanding many aspects of the body, it delayed adding the study of sex and conception.

As physicians assisted women in childbirth, and formal medical education in the nineteenth century came to include obstetrics, the new science gradually began to include women's anatomy and physiology.

In America, the reticence of natural philosophy and medicine about sexuality was broken by freethinkers and advocates for change. A strong believer in the value of empirical science, Frances Wright saw the expression of sexual feeling as a vital part of life, necessary to human happiness (see Documents 4 and 5). If rightly used, sex was a great force; if distorted, moral and physical disease followed. Neither law nor custom but rather a person's knowledge of its consequences was the true regulator of sexual passion.

Wright even diverged from her fellow freethinkers by confronting the issue of race. When she founded Nashoba, a utopian experiment outside of Memphis, Tennessee, in 1825, she sought to educate slaves in the ways of freedom through a scheme that allowed them to work for their emancipation. Forced to defend sexual practices at Nashoba that included interracial intercourse outside of marriage, she argued for the interbreeding of races and a new understanding of sexual relations.

Focusing on Frances Wright helps to remind readers that the subordinate status of two groups—blacks and women—informs all the writings on sex before the Civil War. In the public deliberations about sex after Wright, only a minute fraction of printed material on popular science explicitly engaged race. Yet all of it implicitly did for, unless specified, the described bodies with their reproductive organs and functions were imagined as white. Occasionally, sexual relations across the color line, real or imagined, prompted discussion. When it did, the words were always controversial and often designed to incite opposition. In the writings about sex that follow, women often got equal or even predominant billing with men. But their prominence on the page did not reflect their position in society. Women lived, worked, and loved in a political and legal system of inequality, denied many of the fundamental rights and responsibilities of citizenship. Ministers and moralists assumed that the principal role of women, whatever their own personal aspirations, was to serve as wives and mothers.

Freethinkers were the first open promoters of contraception in the United States. In early 1831, Owen published his *Moral Physiology; or, a Brief and Plain Treatise on the Population Question* (see Document 6), the first American work to offer arguments for decreasing births and practical, though limited, advice on contraception. Owen accepted Wright's position that the reproductive instinct was essentially good. However, he ignored both the racial controversies and the gender inequalities that Wright had engaged, restating many of her positions in language that was both race and gender free. Sexual urges in Owen's view were natural, like hunger and thirst, and their satisfaction a legitimate pleasure. In addition, the reproductive instinct served to draw human beings outside of themselves and toward others.

As did his Enlightenment mentors, Owen found that the source of morality lay in nature and that there was a need to seek measure in the reproductive instinct, as in all things. He brought to his writings the theory of British contemporary Thomas Malthus, that population always outpaces the food supply, but unlike the gloomy economist, Owen looked to economic and social solutions to cure the ills of society. Rather than delaying marriage, Owen urged young couples to practice contraception.

Moral Physiology enjoyed a long career in America, and it encouraged Charles Knowlton, a physician in western Massachusetts, to write and publish *Fruits of Philosophy* (1832), the first book on contraception in the United States based on empirical medical science. It featured the most advanced writing on women's anatomy and reproduction of its time (see Document 7). Knowlton's title alluded to the philosophy he espoused that rejected notions of sin and defined virtue as the temperate satisfaction of natural appetites. Knowlton believed it necessary that sex and sexuality move out of the realm of morality and into that of physiology.

Knowlton subsequently published many editions of *Fruits of Philosophy*. Although his basic message remained the same, in later editions his discussions of the sexual organs and their functions became increasingly explicit. The book had great influence in the United States and England, where its instructions on the douche method of contraception contributed to the falling birth rate. In the United States, over the course of the nineteenth century, the typical number of children born of white women fell from roughly seven per woman to about three and a half. This decrease was most evident among the urban, white middle class whose families had been in America for several generations. The decline in the birthrate occurred for many reasons. One is economic: Children, a valuable resource of labor on a farm, became an expense in the city, and this may have led married couples to seek ways to limit the number of births. Republican Motherhood carried a special responsibility to nurture children carefully and see that they were well educated. New notions of romantic love put feeling and its expression at the center of marriage, and this added to reasons to separate sexual intercourse from conception. While population decline had many causes, to be sure, some nineteenth-century commentators attributed it to the contraceptive knowledge that Knowlton's book imparted.

Together Wright, Owen, and Knowlton created a new literature of sexuality that, beginning in the 1830s, laid part of the foundation for the third framework, the popular science of the body. Books and pamphlets took the term *reform physiology* to designate efforts to describe the reproductive organs and their functions and to prescribe healthful ways of living. In contrast to the vernacular understanding of sex existing within a body of four humors and to religious statements against lust, the new popular science described the body with reference to nerves and brain. Sexual desire—no longer imagined as springing from heated blood—was now in the mind, originating in messages sent from the brain through the nerves. In some cases, contraception became an expressed goal, and texts offered specific techniques to prevent pregnancy.

CHRISTIAN REFORM PHYSIOLOGY

The third framework was divided from the outset. Writers explored the relation of sexuality to new notions of the body, mind, and health, but they struggled over the appropriate words and concepts by which the passions and the reproductive organs and their functions were best understood and explained. Reformers rooted in the Christian tradition added their voices and opinions to those of the freethinkers. Perhaps the most important of these was Sylvester Graham.

The son and grandson of Connecticut clergymen, Graham prepared for the ministry but turned to temperance reform and the lecture circuit. He studied the writings of American physician Benjamin Rush and French physiologists, and their ideas initially led him to develop an understanding of alcohol and all stimulants as irritants to the natural system. In 1832, Graham achieved renown with lectures on the cholera epidemic, published in 1833, that posited a link between illness and sexual expression. In keeping with his era's approach to disease as a sign that the body's systems were overtaxed, he determined that the cause of cholera was bad habits, especially sexual indulgence. He pointed to cholera outbreaks among the poorest and most exploited of American workers, those black and white men who labored to build canals in Washington, D.C., and the Hindi of India, perceiving these peoples as living in cauldrons of sensuality.

Graham expanded his understanding of the body and its sexual functioning in *A Lecture to Young Men* (see Document 8), first delivered in 1832 and published in 1834. In this work, Graham did not discuss explicitly race or social class, but these divisions hovered over his writings nonetheless. The body he addressed in his lecture belonged neither to the canal worker nor to the Indian follower of Hinduism; rather, it belonged to the middle-class white men in his audience. In using universal language but having in mind persons of a specific race and class, Graham's disciples would follow his lead.

Graham argued that there were two kinds of appetites: that for nutrition and that for reproduction. Hunger and thirst, which enabled the individual to survive, required constant appeasement. Reproduction, which allowed the survival of the species, demanded no necessary exercise or satisfaction. Graham regarded nutrition as the most important function of the body and the key to health. The Graham cracker, for which he is remembered today, was an element of his health crusade to return Americans to whole-grain food (although Graham would not have approved of its current sugar content and additives). In Graham's understanding, sexual intercourse created danger and risk to the nervous system, threatening digestion. Because the body could take such stimulation only a few times in its lifetime, Graham urged, for health's sake, sexual restraint in marriage and abstinence outside it.

In Graham's campaign for a series of measures to protect the stomach and calm the passions, diet was the key element. *Aristotle's Master-piece* saw juicy meat and racy wine as adding heat to the body to contribute to the vigor of the sexual embrace; Graham turned to vegetarianism and cold water to cool the body. Moreover, in contrast to the authors of *Aristotle's Master-piece,* who encouraged couples to admire each other's beauty and recite poetry, Graham attempted to discourage mental sources of sexual stimulation. The early nineteenth century was an era of romantic expression in which poems and fiction centered on heightened emotion. With popular science now locating sex in the mind and not in the blood, Graham and his followers emphasized the power of imaginative literature and theater and their potential dangers. Graham's regimen was, simply put, a prescription to dampen lust.

THE MASTURBATION SCARE

Christians who wrote about the popular science of the body were diverted by the masturbation scare. Graham's recommendation for sexual restraint within marriage seemed questionable to many couples, but his campaign against youthful masturbation fell on the open ears

INSANITY.

CONSUMPTION.

ONANISM.

Figure 4. *Masturbation's consequences, ca. 1860.* This illustration demonstrates the belief widely held in the mid-nineteenth century that masturbation led to mental and physical disease.

Boston Medical Library in the Francis A. Countway Library of Medicine.

of countless parents. Given Graham's comprehension of the body and the power of sexual excitement, it is understandable that he regarded masturbation in the young as a particular danger (see Document 9). Often beginning early in life when bodily organs were still undeveloped, children started a habit of masturbation that, in Graham's mind, destroyed body and mind and led to early death (see Figure 4). In alarming tones, he spoke and wrote against a practice that he found to be extraordinarily common among boys.

Other writers took up Graham's cause against masturbation. Books authored by such writers as Luther V. Bell and Mary S. Gove proliferated, counseling parents and describing a youthful sexual culture that was especially worrisome to adults at a time when more and more boys and girls left home for school and work. Bell was a physician and one of the founders of psychiatry in the United States. As medical superintendent of the McLean Asylum for the Insane near Boston, he was particularly impressed by the annual reports of Samuel Bayard Woodward, the superintendent of the State Hospital for Lunatics in Worcester, Massachusetts, which chronicled the masturbation practices of inmates.

Bell, like many others, wrote his book to warn young men of evils brought to body and mind by masturbation (see Document 10). Gove, who began her career as a follower of Sylvester Graham, became a lecturer and writer on the body to a largely female audience (see Document 11). Bell and Gove joined a host of others whose writings against masturbation targeted the emerging middle class in a society being transformed by commercialization, industrialization, urbanization, and education. During this era, it was a rare person, such as Charles Knowlton, who offered a different point of view (see Document 12).

If writers such as Graham, Bell, and Gove are to be believed, masturbation became a significant source of anxiety in the antebellum years. What accounts for its power in the public deliberations of sex during this period? For one thing, discussions of masturbation dealt with childhood sexuality. In an age that romanticized childhood innocence, these writings described a world in which youths and adults introduced 'children to sexual acts and children introduced them to each other. Moreover, the narratives in these writings allowed for dark forces in human beings that defied reason and understanding. As in Gothic literature, writers on masturbation explored the realm of powers that seemed beyond human will. Young men and women with every advantage sickened, became deranged, did evil, and died.

Perhaps the most important reason for masturbation's inclusion in the conversation, however, was the great change coming over middling folk as they became middle class. Their primary responsibility to their offspring became education, both socialization and formal schooling. Their real legacy was less the transfer of property than what they left in their children's heads. Mothers, now given an enhanced role as "Mothers of the Republic," were the special guardians of the young. This was particularly true for the group most involved in generating—and probably reading—the literature on masturbation in these years, white middle-class Northerners. Writings on masturbation addressed those who sought to be conscientious parents. They wanted advice about how to raise their children. How could they ensure their children's morality? How could they guide them, especially when their sons and daughters were studying in school or working in the city?

Middle-class parents, investing in the education of their children, experienced a tension: On the one hand, they wanted their children to succeed in the world; on the other hand, they hoped their offspring would retain the values of home. In contrast to agrarian parents who governed their sons and daughters with the promise of an inheritance of land or dowry, those in the nineteenth-century middle class enjoyed far less control over their children. Try as parents might, boys and girls could go wrong. They could become wayward artists instead of disciplined workers, they could withdraw from the company of others, or they could deviate from adult notions of respectable behavior. Parents who feared for their children craved reassurance. If they failed, and their children went astray, they needed something to blame. Although writing about masturbation addressed many middle-class concerns, perhaps above all else it spoke to parental anxiety about their children and the future.

Discussion of masturbation was a part of the larger consideration of sex in the antebellum years that treated questions of sex, desire, reproduction, contraception, and health. In the 1830s and 1840s, these were expressed in one of three frameworks. Vernacular sexuality accepted sexual pleasure and, for women, attended to the control of fertility. Evangelical Christianity castigated men and women for their carnal natures. Reform physiology offered a popular science of the body that reinterpreted sexuality. This third framework included freethinkers as well as Christians, both groups thinking about scientific notions of the body and health but offering different prescriptions for wholesome living.

NEW VOICES AT MID-CENTURY

By mid-century a new generation of writers emerged, carrying forward the clashing perspectives of Christian reformer Graham and the freethinking Knowlton and adding new insights. They wrote in an era of changing medical practice in which many contending medical branches explored alternative approaches to the body and vied for practitioners and believers. Most of the writers of reform physiology were medical irregulars: they wrote for a broader audience at a time in which the regulars, or traditional physicians, normally wrote only for each other in medical journals. The irregulars typically used the language of democracy, arguing for the right to spread physiological knowledge to a wide audience. Although they disagreed with each other and orthodox physicians on treatment and on the medical theories underlying it, many irregulars agreed with other doctors that the age was troubled by ill health and that sickness was an evil to be eliminated.

The health reformer William Andrus Alcott carried on the tradition of Sylvester Graham. A teacher, physician, and writer, Alcott preached ways of healthy living in many books over a long career (see Document 13). He was a leading exponent of sexual restraint in marriage. Alcott's position was a powerful one in his era. Many of his prescriptions, if not his understanding of the body, were also held by phrenologists in the antebellum years.

Phrenology was regarded in its era as one of the alternative forms of medicine. In 1832, Orson Squire Fowler converted to phrenology after hearing a lecture on the theory of the Viennese physician Franz Joseph Gall that the brain was made up of separate parts, each governing a specific aspect of character (see Figure 5). Joined by his brother Lorenzo and other family members, Orson Fowler created a vast array of enterprises designed to spread phrenological wisdom across the nation; the Fowler brothers' many books sold widely (see Documents 14, 15, and 16).

Phrenology located cognitive, emotional, and sensory capacities in distinct areas of the brain. According to its tenets, the reproductive instinct or sexual feeling was rooted in the organ of "amativeness" in the cerebellum. Positioned at the base of the skull above the nape of the neck, it stood thus at the link between the brain and the spinal column, the governing center of the nervous system. Initially phrenology attempted to place itself outside the divide between the Christian Grahamites and the freethinkers. As its practitioners tried to accommodate science and its understanding of human reproduction, they nonetheless showed traces of the evangelical milieu from which they had sprung. When they embraced the sexual as "natural," they did so with fear and hesitation. Although the Fowlers ultimately declared that sexual passion was legitimate, God-given, and appropriate to women as well as men, they hedged their bets. Much of their writing blended enthusiasm for marriage and sexual passion with conventional notions about women and an appreciation of the value of sexual moderation similar to those of Alcott.

Unlike the Fowlers, Frederick Hollick's links were to the freethinking tradition, not to Christianity or Graham. A lecturer and medical practitioner who had immigrated to the United States to be part of Robert Dale Owen's utopian experiment in New Harmony, Indiana, Hollick wrote popular books on reproduction and physiology for a wide audience (see Documents 17 and 18). As had Owen before him, Hollick argued for the positive value of sexual feeling. Not only was it neither immoral nor injurious, it was the basis for morality and society. Hollick understood sexual sensibility in terms of the nervous system, as did Graham, but much of his writing on sexual response recalled *Aristotle's Master-piece*. In many ways, Hollick was a sexual enthusiast. He believed that as the sexual organs matured, all persons experienced sexual feelings, although to varying degrees. He advocated early marriage and regular sexual intercourse. Although he did not comment on frequency, he argued against "undue continence," stating

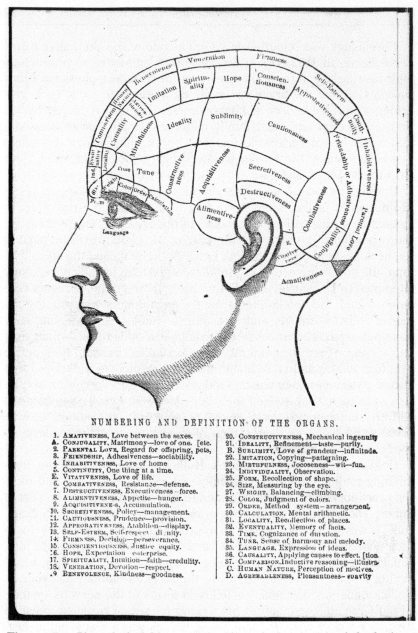

NUMBERING AND DEFINITION OF THE ORGANS.

1. AMATIVENESS, Love between the sexes.
A. CONJUGALITY, Matrimony—love of one. [etc.
2. PARENTAL LOVE, Regard for offspring, pets,
3. FRIENDSHIP, Adhesiveness—sociability.
4. INHABITIVENESS, Love of home
5. CONTINUITY, One thing at a time.
E. VITATIVENESS, Love of life.
6. COMBATIVENESS, Resistance—defense.
7. DESTRUCTIVENESS, Executiveness—force.
8. ALIMENTIVENESS, Appetite—hunger.
9. ACQUISITIVENESS, Accumulation.
10. SECRETIVENESS, Policy—management.
11. CAUTIOUSNESS, Prudence—provision.
12. APPROBATIVENESS, Ambition—display.
13. SELF-ESTEEM, Self-respect—dignity.
14. FIRMNESS, Decision—perseverance.
15. CONSCIENTIOUSNESS, Justice equity.
16. HOPE, Expectation enterprise.
17. SPIRITUALITY, Intuition—faith—credulity.
18. VENERATION, Devotion—respect.
19. BENEVOLENCE, Kindness—goodness.
20. CONSTRUCTIVENESS, Mechanical ingenuity
21. IDEALITY, Refinement—taste—purity.
B. SUBLIMITY, Love of grandeur—infinitude.
22. IMITATION, Copying—patterning.
23. MIRTHFULNESS, Jocoseness—wit—fun.
24. INDIVIDUALITY, Observation.
25. FORM, Recollection of shape.
26. SIZE, Measuring by the eye.
27. WEIGHT, Balancing—climbing.
28. COLOR, Judgment of colors.
29. ORDER, Method system—arrangement
30. CALCULATION, Mental arithmetic.
31. LOCALITY, Recollection of places.
32. EVENTUALITY, Memory of facts.
33. TIME, Cognizance of duration.
34. TUNE, Sense of harmony and melody.
35. LANGUAGE, Expression of ideas.
36. CAUSALITY, Applying causes to effect. [tion.
37. COMPARISON, Inductive reasoning—illustra-
C. HUMAN NATURE, Perception of motives.
D. AGREEABLENESS, Pleasantness—suavity

Figure 5. *Phrenological Map, 1859.* Phrenologists imagined the brain as divided into separate parts, each of which had control over a specific element of character. Amativeness, or "love between the sexes," held an important place at the base of the skull, linking the spinal cord to the brain.

From *New Illustrated Self-Instructor in Phrenology and Physiology* (New York: Fowler and Wells, Publishers, 1859).

20

that it produced ill health and unhappiness. He argued that women normally did experience sexual feeling and ought always to do so for the sake of health and good spirits.

Sex at the Center of Life

By the 1850s, writers at the far reaches of reform physiology, most notably Mary Gove and Thomas Low Nichols, had placed sex at the center of life (see Documents 19 and 20). Sexual experimentation had come to play an important role in a number of religious, reform, and utopian movements. Spiritualism in particular was drawing great numbers. Spiritualists' belief in communicating with the dead and in an afterlife that continued the one on earth led some of them to emphasize spiritual affinity with a mate. In an odd twist of this doctrine, a few adherents publicly rejected their earthly husbands and wives and sought divorce or took lovers. Drawing on these movements, Gove and Nichols were heralds of the fourth framework for the public deliberation of sex. Their collective voice in the sexual conversation combined visionary and radical politics with notions of sexual liberty and freedom of expression.

Believing that sex lay at the core of being, Gove and Nichols held that sexual expression in heterosexual intercourse was the most vital facet of life, as important for women as for men. They asserted that because sex was so valuable to the self, it must be freely expressed. Any diversion or repression of sexual urges from their "natural expression" in coition was harmful.

The two present a complicated case. Their coauthored writings straddle the worlds of Grahamite doctrines and medicine on the one hand and those on the other of journalism and sensational fiction, to be considered later in this section. In her early career, Mary Gove had been a follower of Sylvester Graham, speaking about issues relating to the body and masturbation to a largely female audience. In the 1840s, she ran a water-cure boarding house and wrote fiction. In 1848, she married Thomas Low Nichols, a man five years her junior.[4] Nichols was a newspaperman and writer with ties to New York's rough world. After marrying Gove, he studied medicine at the University of the City of New York (later New York University), and upon graduation in 1850 used "M.D." after his name. With their marriage, Gove and Nichols engaged in an important and controversial collaboration. Enthusiasts for a range of reforms, the two were part of New York's radical circle and considered themselves to be Spiritualists. They produced a spate of reform writing, including the two books *Esoteric Anthropology* and *Marriage.*

Nichols and Gove operated for a time the Reform Bookstore in New York City, which oversaw the printing of *Esoteric Anthropology.* Much of their work was reprinted by commercial publishers. By mid-century, an alternative publishing network for material on health and the body had come into being, with its own bookstores, imprints, and periodicals. An alliance of sorts was forged between authors writing in a reformist genre and commercially viable alternative publishing houses that understood that there was a market for books informing the public about the physiology and politics of sex.

Esoteric Anthropology was Nichols's most influential work, and it went into seven editions over the course of nine years following publication. His enthusiasm for sexual expression appears in language more often found in fiction than in works on physiology. Gove likely served as coauthor of sections of the book, contributing many of the ideas on physiology that came from Graham. *Esoteric Anthropology* was an extraordinary book, set apart from other works of its day by its rhapsodic passages, detail, and emphasis on physicality. The book treated male and female homosexuality explicitly. In key places, *Esoteric Anthropology* celebrated the delights of the "sexual embrace" and attempted to describe orgasm. Although this book never used the term "free love," or sexual union outside of marriage, an informal section responding to questions advocated it. The Nichols's openly collaborative book, *Marriage,* did discuss free love, explicitly, with each author taking a different position.

After announcing in 1857 that they were converting to Catholicism, Gove and Nichols immigrated with their daughter to England at the start of the Civil War and remained abroad for the rest of their lives. They left an ambiguous and ambitious legacy. Unusual in their explicitness, treatment of women's sexual response, and considerations of homosexuality, they gathered and partially summarized much of the information available in the physiological and reform literature about sex and reproduction. Their writing blurred the boundaries between the physiological and the racy. They intertwined physiological discussion with advocacy of free love. Living at the edge of many social movements that challenged the relation between sex and marriage in word and deed, Gove and Nichols were the most important early voices of the fourth framework, which put sex at the center of life.

Gove and Nichols spoke and wrote at a moment when social change was visible in American cities. The penny press and flash papers announced a new world of sexual possibility. At the same time, book-sellers, seeking a wider audience, advertised physiological works along-side sensational novels, traditional erotica, and outright pornography. Simultaneously, the marketing of birth control and abortion services obfuscated the line between advice and commerce.

CONTROVERSY AND COMMERCE

Many saw that the world was changing in antebellum America. One of the surest signs of this transformation was the new penny press, sold daily on city streets. Creators of the modern news story, these dailies offered sensationalism and advertisements that reflected novel ele-ments in urban sexual culture. As women became literate in increas-ing numbers, they constituted a new audience for public prints and a fresh market. As they moved into the city in search of work, women broke links with their female face-to-face communities of family and neighborhood. This disruption of community knowledge created the demand for the dissemination of printed information on abortion and the rise of female abortionists in cities like New York. Just as mental hospitals took the place of homes in the care of the mentally ill, so abortionists moved in to provide services that the women's commu-nity once offered its members. Advertisements by abortionists, in-cluding those of Ann Trow Lohman as Madame Restell, beginning in 1838, spread the word about how to obtain these services (see Docu-ment 21). In this way, elements of ordinary women's sexual culture, focusing on ways to prevent conception and terminate unwanted preg-nancies, entered the public realm. By mid-century, some physicians and many moral reformers were publicly opposing abortion.

Another visible source of change in American cities was the grow-ing society of sporting men. They constituted a diverse group. At the core were men for whom games were a means of gaining a living—gamblers, con men, and organizers of prize fights. Surrounding them were their various admirers, who included journeymen, college stu-dents, wealthy men "on the town," and young clerks who had come to the city from rural and small-town America. Sporting men made up a loose fellowship that sought pleasure and actively resisted pressures to conform to middle-class standards. They believed that a man with money to spend could take his enjoyment where he could find it, with-out thought of consequences or obligations. In their minds, women were merely instruments of men's pleasure to be used and discarded

Figure 6. New-York by Gas-Light: Hooking a Victim, *Lithograph by Serrell and Perkins, ca. 1850.* Well-dressed prostitutes are shown soliciting business, seeking to attract gentlemen in front of a restaurant on an urban street. In this era, prostitution was an important part of the urban scene and became a significant public issue.

New York by Gas Light, Hooking a Victim, c.1850 (litho), American School, (19th century)/© Museum of the City of New York, USA/The Bridgeman Art Library.

freely. Thus for a sporting man with money to spend, the prostitute was the perfect imagined sexual object (see Figure 6). Commercial establishments arose to cater to men's tastes, providing theaters, saloons, brothels, and improvised gambling dens and prize-fight rings.

Two incidents brought sporting life under public scrutiny. (See Figure 7.) The first began in the 1830s, when a campaign of moral reform targeted prostitutes and, to a lesser degree, their clients. In 1829 Charles Grandison Finney came to New York City to stir up revival enthusiasm, increasing the pressure for good works. In his wake, the American Tract Society, an evangelical Christian association, brought in John R. McDowall, a young urban missionary. In 1831, McDowall issued the *Magdalen Report* (see Document 22), which presented the public with information about prostitution and stressed the need for reform. The second started in 1841, when a number of racy weeklies written for sporting men or those who aspired to join their company, appeared in New York. Following the financial panic of 1837 many

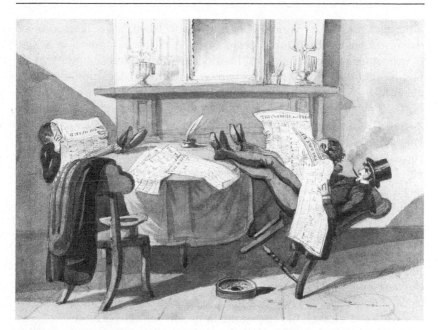

Figure 7. Reading Room of the Astor House, *Watercolor and Ink by Nicolino Calyo, 1840.* Fashionable young men put their feet up and smoke as they read the daily papers. This image conveys something of the jauntiness and the defiance of middle-class manners that fed into the emergence of a male sporting culture.

Astor House Reading Room, 1840 (w/c on paper), Calyo, Nicolino (1799–1884)/© Museum of the City of New York, USA/The Bridgeman Art Library.

writers sought new ways of earning a living. A few of them created the "flash" or sporting press. Taking such titles as the *Sunday Flash,* the *Whip and Satirist of New-York and Brooklyn,* and the *Rake,* these papers focused on many popular entertainments and commercial establishments but gave special attention to brothel life (see Documents 23 through 27).

On its masthead, the *Whip,* for example, presented itself to its potential readers as "Devoted to the Sports of the Ring, the Turf, and City Life — such as Sprees, Larks, Crim. Cons, Seductions, Rapes, &c. — not forgetting to keep a watchful eye on all Brothels and their frail inmates." In its pages it offered a regular column, "Sketches of Characters" that portrayed urban types, especially men about town and the women they might encounter, under clever engravings often of a suggestive nature. Perspectives on prostitutes were multiple, representing in part the different interests of writers and, perhaps, individual ambivalences. In its various "Walks About Town," the *Whip* offered the results of brothel tours, evaluating the different houses in a kind of consumer guide for readers. In short articles, it and the other weeklies frequently celebrated well-known prostitutes, treating them like celebrities. Nominally dedicated to reform, the weeklies offered exposés, typically negative portrayals of older brothel madams. However, a "frail one" or a "nymph" (two euphemisms for a prostitute) who was young and beautiful, was generally accorded at the minimum the respect due a victim and at the maximum the admiration due royalty. Although a weekly might indulge in the familiar "seduced-and-abandoned" story, such as the tale of Amanda Green in "Lives of the Nymphs" (see Document 23), it suggestively played with the seduction scenes with hints and winks, unlike usual publications that offered narratives of victimization.

Despite the content of its papers, the flash press claimed to have moral purposes, especially when faced with criticism. Editors took on the language of outrage and reform in dealing with abortionists, such as Madame Restell. They policed the racial divide by castigating others with the charge of "amalgamation," or sexual relations between white and black. In addition, their words became particularly shrill in dealing with male violators of heterosexual codes, those whom they called sodomites. It is likely that homosexuality was perceived as a special threat to this male world that celebrated the lustful pleasures of brothel sex.

Almost immediately, some people tried to police the flash papers through the courts. Prosecutors invoked the common law of obscene libel. As many articles about prostitutes and men on the town came under legal scrutiny, editors of the flash press learned that those in authority in New York City did not openly share the culture of sporting men — at least not when they were in public view. Juries ruled the publications obscene, and judges sentenced the papers' owners to prison terms of thirty or sixty days. The court records do not contain the efforts of the editors to defend themselves, but their weekly papers offered opportunity for them to present their arguments. Typically they alleged that the original libel charges had been the result of personal vendettas, and they proclaimed their innocence of all wrongdoing. They slammed opponents and insisted that their sheets were put forward as a means of bringing about moral reform. William Joseph Snelling, once a well-regarded poet, fulminated about the wrongs of legal proceedings against him. Posing as a reformer, he sought to put his treatment of prostitutes in a moral light and insisted that he did not create but only exposed the evil that existed. He argued that his writing was coarse only to his accusers and that to call his writings into question threatened the publication of great literary works. A few years later, another of the imprisoned editors offered a defense that questioned the common-law principles that criminalized words, not deeds.

More well-off editors might have withstood these penalties and returned to fight another round, but the men involved in the flash weeklies had little capital reserves. They served their time and went on to other pursuits. In 1845, George Wilkes, one of their number, founded the *National Police Gazette,* a weekly that carried much of the spirit of the 1840s flash press into the twentieth century.

By mid-century, the commercial side of the sexual conversation was finding new material and new outlets. Traditionally some American printers and sellers of erotica marketed books and prints imported from Europe where sexual accusation had long been used to delegitimize those in power, such as kings and priests. During and following the French Revolution there had been an outpouring of erotic prints from France and England, much of it politically inspired. New opportunities emerged for erotica and pornography in its own right, and America appeared to be a waiting market. In an effort to stem the growing traffic in erotic prints, the federal government exercised its power in one of the limited ways it had available, the regulation of foreign trade. In 1842, in Section 28 of the Tariff Act, Congress prohibited the importation of all "indecent and obscene prints, paintings, lithographs, engravings, and transparencies." Any such matter could be "proceeded against, seized, and forfeited, by due course of law, and the said articles shall be forthwith destroyed." The prohibition was immediately enforced in the courts.

Its ironic effect, however, was to stimulate publishers in the United States to reproduce European works for the American market. International copyrights were not secure in the United States, and, even if they were, copyright protection did not extend to works that courts judged obscene. Earlier in the nineteenth century, British author John Cleland's *Memoirs of a Woman of Pleasure* or *Fanny Hill* had been printed and distributed in the United States, but this was a rather modest endeavor compared to what followed. After the 1842 Tariff Act, erotic books printed domestically entered the American market, and American writers were encouraged to produce homegrown works. So much for the efforts of early federal legislation to regulate American morality.

Changes in the organization and technology of printing and new modes of distribution made published materials cheaper and more widely distributed. Prices fell as expensive machinery—stereotypes and steam-powered presses—took the place of men. By the late 1840s, periodical depots emerged in major cities, blending publishing and selling. The transportation revolution, especially the railroads, allowed increasing concentration of book manufacture in eastern cities, especially New York City. Following the lead of the British, some American printers bought failing newspapers and, using their format and ability to take advantage of lower postal rates than books, created story papers and pamphlet novels, typically referred to as paper- or yellow-covered books. Fiction, once reserved for those who could pay two dollars a novel—the middle and upper classes—was now available to a mass audience at six cents for a story paper or twenty-five cents for a pamphlet book.

Some of this new fiction was sold alongside the old, accompanied by physiological texts. One can see this in the advertisement of P. F. Harris in the *Broadway Belle* (see Document 28). Seeking to attract a wider audience, Harris bundled together physiological works, commercial erotica, and sensational novels. For a time, Harris published the works of George Thompson, the most prolific American author of sensational fiction in the 1840s and 1850s. His novels, if such they can be called, allow access into the minds of their typical readers. Thompson's principal urban subjects were the adventures of sporting men and the contrasts of wealth and poverty in the city.

Thompson's works followed the path of other writers in his period, taking the reader up and down the class system in the varied districts of New York City. In *The Mysteries of Bond Street; or, The Seraglios of Upper Tendom* (see Document 29), Thompson introduced the reader to characters who move through various neighborhoods, especially the high-class end of the wealthiest parts of New York and the low-class end of the poorest, the area known as Five Points. Thompson salted his tale with violence, sexual titillation, and scenes of opulence. What often propelled a Thompson story was the desire to exact revenge after sexual betrayal. Thompson worked within the unmasking tradition of the flash press and, like many of its writers, used the language of outrage.

To novels such as those by Thompson, booksellers added a new and more varied literature of contraception. By the 1850s, entrepreneurs were eager to make money by offering new techniques of contraception for sale. In promoting their products in books and pamphlets,

they stated their rationales for sexual expression divorced from reproduction, adding to existing print discussions of the physiology of sexual intercourse and sexual pleasure. In *Henry's Private Adviser,* for
example, Dr. J. Henry of Rossville, Maryland, sought to sell his "Chart
of Life," a guide to what is today called the rhythm method of contraception (see Document 30). In his sheet, he offered a broad justifica-
tion for birth control. Although Dr. Henry distributed his sheet as a
newspaper, some contraceptive guidance was marketed alongside sensational novels and traditional erotica.

In 1857, commercially available erotica hit a new phase when
George Ackerman published *Venus' Miscellany* under the business
name James Ramerio. In contrast to the flash weeklies of the 1840s
that specialized in vilification and gossip about prostitutes, this weekly
contained fiction that was much more sexually explicit (see Document 31). As in many works of erotica designed for a male audience in
the antebellum years, the focus was on describing women's experience of passion. Ackerman also used the name James Ramerio for
publishing many racy books, including those of George Thompson,
along with a few familiar European titles and reprints of *Aristotle's
Master-piece.* Ackerman advertised these books as "Rich, Rare and
Racy Reading" in his weekly *Venus' Miscellany.* He took "Jean
Rosseau" as the business name for his pornography and other products marketed "To the Sporting Fraternity" (see Document 32).

CODA: THE COMSTOCK LAW OF 1873

The sexual crosscurrents of mid-century and the rise in commerce in
erotica, works of physiology, and outright pornography swirled around
evangelical Christian laymen in New York, especially those business-
men leading the Young Men's Christian Association (Y.M.C.A.). They
especially feared the sexual dangers faced by the young man in the
city. Originally schooled in the sexual framework spread by the Second Great Awakening, they shared the obsessive fear of masturbation
of such Christian reform physiologists as Sylvester Graham and
Luther Bell. Beginning in the 1850s, Y.M.C.A. leaders pursued material they regarded as "obscene," especially the type of pornography
typified by fiction in *Venus' Miscellany.* In this period, authorities did
not go after most materials that dealt with sexual knowledge, even
those that were written in a racy style or that advocated birth control
or free love.

The target of prosecution changed after the Civil War. In 1873, prodded by the Y.M.C.A. of New York, Congress passed the federal law for the "Suppression of Trade in, and Circulation of, Obscene Literature and Articles of Immoral Use" (see Document 33). The statute made it illegal and punishable by either fines or imprisonment or both to send through the mail a wide range of sexually explicit materials, including contraceptive information and advertisements for abortion. The bill gave judges the power to issue warrants for search and seizure. In Washington, D.C., and the territories, places where the federal government had direct jurisdiction, the act also made it a misdemeanor, punishable by fine and imprisonment, to sell such materials. Anthony Comstock, the representative of the Y.M.C.A. of New York who lobbied for the bill in Washington, became its chief enforcer as a special agent of the U.S. Post Office. Upon its passage, the bill became known as the Comstock Law. Many states wrote "Little Comstock" laws that mirrored the 1873 federal statute, prohibiting the same sales that the federal law made illegal in the District of Columbia and the territories.

Until 1873, most materials that dealt with sexual knowledge, even those outlining contraceptive techniques or supporting free love, such as the works by Mary Gove and Thomas Low Nichols, were purchased and read freely. Enforcement in the courts of the 1873 Comstock Law and state Little Comstock laws changed that, sending booksellers and publishers to jail for selling or mailing a wide range of sexually explicit materials. These materials included those works written in a scientific manner that offered sex education or contraceptive guidance. Some publishers bent to the wind and excised racy passages or information about contraception; some ceased publication; some merely went underground to await a different day. With the passage of the Comstock Law, a new era in public deliberation of sex began.

Beginning in the 1870s, opponents of suppression, motivated by belief in the importance of sexual expression and by commitment to freedom of speech, created a vital countertradition. In the twentieth century, their words were strengthened by the redefined power of the First Amendment to guarantee the freedom of speech of citizens against the power of the state. Linked to pressures from commercial culture to keep markets unfettered, these beliefs in the importance of sex and the First Amendment led to a critical weakening of the Comstock Law. Over the last four decades or so, the U.S. Supreme Court has curtailed the legal power once assumed by Comstock, the post office, and the other public censors of sexual materials.

Yet today, many issues pertaining to sex are still unresolved. American society is profoundly divided over questions of morality, its relation to government, and the rights of free speech. The daily news brings reports of contemporary clashes over medical research, gay marriage, abortion, museum exhibitions, public funding of scholarship, sex education in the schools, and censorship of the Internet. Although much separates the early twenty-first century from the nineteenth, under the surface of technological change, many of the profound issues that Americans grappled with in that earlier era remain our own.

NOTES

[1] This introduction is based on my *Rereading Sex: Battles over Sexual Knowledge and Suppression in Nineteenth-Century America* (New York: Alfred A. Knopf, 2002; Vintage, paperback, 2003). Full documentation can be found in that work.

[2] The use of the word *framework* rather than the more fashionable academic word *discourse* is intentional. *Discourse* may cause some readers to assume a seamless link between ideas about sexuality and sexual practice, that people read works that completely define their feelings and shape their behavior. *Discourse* is perhaps most often associated with the work of Michel Foucault; although he always allowed a dialectical process, in which a prohibition calls forth an incitement, my own conception involves a more fluid, even disorderly composition of elements. A good treatment of these issues is the preface to Thomas W. Laqueur, *Making Sex: Body and Gender from the Greeks to Freud* (Cambridge, Mass.: Harvard University Press, 1990).

[3] Cornelia Hughes Dayton, "Taking the Trade: Abortion and Gender Relations in an Eighteenth-Century New England Village," *William and Mary Quarterly* 48 (1991): 24–25.

[4] Although she changed her name when she married Nichols, for clarity I continue to refer to her as Mary Gove.

The Documents

PART TWO

The Documents

1

Voices in the Sexual Conversation: The Four Frameworks

The First Framework: Vernacular Sexuality

1

From *Aristotle's Master-piece*
1741

First printed in English in 1684, Aristotle's Master-piece *offers a view into vernacular sexuality, the first framework for the public deliberation of sex. Taking the name of Aristotle to lend authority, this anonymously written work contained medical information from many different sources, including popular folklore. It was the most common guide to reproduction and sexual matters in America in the eighteenth and early nineteenth centuries. In keeping with medical thought at the time, the body is seen as governed by the four fluids (or humors). Blood combined with heat was the source of sexual desire. Man was the hotter, drier, and lustier sex; woman, the cooler and moister. Women's anatomy and desire were etched along the lines of a one-sex model, in which a woman is a man outside-in.*

It is strange to see how Things that are common are slighted for that very Reason, tho' in themselves worthy of the most serious Consideration: And this is the very Case, as to the Subject we are now to treat

---

Aristotle's Works Compleated in Four Parts, containing 1. the Compleat Master-piece (London: Printed, and Sold by the Booksellers, ca. 1741).

of. What is there more common than the Begetting of Children? And yet what is there more wonderful and mysterious than the plastic Power of Nature, by which they are form'd? . . .

The Unfolding of the plastic Power of Nature, in the secret Workings of Generation, and the Formation of the Seed in the Womb, is the Subject of the following Treatise; a Subject so necessary to be known by all the Female Sex, (the Conception of Bearing of Children, being what Nature has ordained their Province) that many for want of this Knowledge have perish'd, with the Fruit of the Womb also; who, had they but understood the Secrets of Generation, which are display'd in this Book, might have been still in the Land of the Living, for the Sake of such therefore have I compiled this Treatise, which I shall divide into Two Parts; in each of which I shall observe this Method. In the First Part I shall,

First, Shew that Nature has no need to be asham'd of any of her Works, give a particular Description of the Parts or Organs of Generation in Men, and afterwards in Women, and then shew the Use of these Parts in the Act of Coition, and how oppositely Nature has adapted them to the End for which she has ordained them.

Secondly, I shall shew the Prohibition or Restriction, that the Creator of all Things, and the Lord of Nature has put upon Man, by the Institution of Marriage; with the Advantage it brings to Mankind.

Thirdly, I shall shew when either Sex may enter into a married State, and be fit to answer the Ends of the Creation, &c.

Fourthly, I shall discourse of Virginity; and therein shew what it is, how it is known, by what means it may be lost, and how a Person may know that it is so, &c.

In the Second Part, (which chiefly relates to married Women; and the Preservation of the Fruit of their Womb, for the Propagation of Mankind to the World) I shall shew.

First, What Conception is; what is pre-requisite thereunto; how a Woman may know when she hath conceived, and whether a Boy or Girl.

Secondly, Shew how a Woman that has conceived, ought to order herself.

Thirdly, Shew what a Woman ought to do that is near the Time of her delivery, and how she ought to be then assisted.

Fourthly, I shall shew what are the Obstructions of Conception; and therein discourse largely about Barrenness,[1] and shew what are the Causes and Cure thereof, both in Men and Women.

[1]The inability to bear offspring; sterility.

Fifthly, Direct Midwife how they shall assist Women in the Time of their Lying in: Bringing several other material Matters, proper to be spoken of under each of those several Heads; which will sufficiently render this Book what *Aristotle* design'd it, his *Compleat Master-piece.*

Chap. I. A particular Description of the Parts, or Instruments of Generation, both in Men or Women

T[h]ough the Instruments, are Parts of Generation in all Creatures, with respect to their outward Form, are not perhaps the more comely, yet, in Compensation of that, Nature has put upon them a more abundant and far greater Honour than on other Parts, in that it has ordained them to be the Means by which every Species of Being is continued

S. 1. Of the Instruments of Generation in Man, with a particular Descrip tion thereof.

from one Generation to another: And therefore, though a Man or Woman were, through the Bounty of Nature, endued with most Angelick Countenances, and the most exact Symmetry and Proportion of Parts, that concurred together to the making up of a most perfect Beauty: yet, if they were defective in the Instruments of Generation, they would not, for all their Beauty, be acceptable either to the other Sex; because they would be thereby render'd uncapable of satisfying the natural Propensions[2] which every one finds in themselves: And this methinks should be sufficient to shew the great Honour Nature has put upon them. And therefore, since it is our Duty to be acquainted with ourselves, and to search out the Wonder of God in Nature, I need not make any Apology for anatomizing the secret Parts of Generation.

The Organ of Generation in Man, Nature has plac'd obvious to the Sight, and is called the Yard, and because hanging without the Belly, is called the *Penis, a Pendendo:* It is in Form long, round, and on the upper Side flattish, and consist of Skin, Tendons, Veins, Arteries, and Sinews, being seated under the *Ossa Pubis,* and ordained by Nature of a two-fold work, viz. For the evacuating of Urine, and conveying the Seed into the Matrix. . . .

The two nervous Bodies; These are called so from their being surrounded with a thick, white, nervous Membrane, tho' their inward Substance is spungy, as consisting principally of Veins, Arteries, and nervous Fibres, interwoven together, like a knit. And Nature has so ordered it, that when the Nerves are fill'd with animal Spirits, and the Arteries with hot and spirituous Blood, then the Yard is distended, and becomes erect? But when the Flux of the Spirits ceases, then the

---

[2]Inclinations or leanings.

Blood, and the remaining Spirits are absorb'd, or suck up by the Veins, and so the *Penis* becomes limber and slaggy. . . .

The Glans, which is at the End of the *Penis,* [is] covered with a very thin Membrane, by reason of which it is of a most exquisite Feeling. It is covered with a *Preputium* or Fore skin, which, in some covers the Top of the Yard quite close, in others not; and by its moving up and down in the Act of Copulation brings Pleasure both to the Man and Woman. . . .

What I have hitherto said relates to the Yard, properly so call'd, but because there are some *Appendices* belonging thereto, which, when wanting, render the Yard of no Use in the Act of Generation, it will also be necessary, before I conclude this Section, to say something of them; I mean the Stones or Testicles, so called because they testify the Person to be a Man. Their Number and Place is obvious; and as to their Use, in them the Blood brought thither by the Spermatick Arteries, is elaborated into Seed.[3] . . .

> And thus Man's noble Parts describ'd we see,
> For such the Parts of Generation be;
> And they that carefully surveys, will find,
> Each Part is fitted for the Use design'd:
> The purest Blood, we find, if well we heed,
> Is in the Testicles turn'd into Seed:
> Why by most proper Channels is transmitted
> Into the Place by Nature for it fitted:
> With highest Sense of Pleasure to excite
> In amorous Combatants the more Delight.
> For Nature does in this great Work design
> Profit and Pleasure, in one Act to join.

WOMAN, next to Man, the noblest Piece of the Creation, is Bone of his Bone of his Bone, and Flesh of his Flesh, a sort of Second self: And in a married State are accounted but one. . . .

It is therefore the secret Parts of that curious piece of Nature that we are to lay open, which we shall do with as much Modesty and Sobriety as will consist with our speaking intelligibly: For 'tis better to say nothing, than to speak so as not to be understood.

S. 2. The Secret parts in Women, appropriated to the Work of generation.

---

[3]According to the bodily knowledge of this text, the body's fluids were interchangeable, and in his testicles a man's heat turned his red blood into white semen.

The external Parts, commonly call'd *Pudenda,* (from the Shame-facedness that is in Women to have them seen) are the Lips of the great Orifice, which are visible to the Eye, and in those that are grown, are cover'd with Hair, and have pretty store of spungy Fat, their Use being to keep the internal Parts from all Annoyance by out-ward Accidents.

Within these are the *Nymphae,* or Wings, which present them-selves to the Eye, when the Lips are severed, and consist of soft and spungy Flesh, and the doubling of the skin plac'd as the sides of the Neck: they compass the *Clytoris,* and both in Form and Col-our, resemble the Comb of a Cock, looking fresh and red, and in the Act of Coition receive the *Penis* or Yard between them: besides which, they give Passage both to the Birth and Urine. The Use of the Wings and Knobs, like Myrtle Berries, shutting the Orifice and Neck of the Bladder, and by the swelling up, cause Titillation and De-light in those Parts, and also obstruct the involuntary Passage of the Urine.

The next Thing is the *Clytoris,* which is a sinewy and hard Part of the Womb, repleat with spungy and black Matter within, in the same manner as the Side-ligaments of the Yard: and indeed resemble it in Form, suffers Erection, and Falling in the same Manner, and it both stirs up Lust, and gives delight in Copulation; For without this, the Fair Sex neither desire martial [*sic*] Embraces, nor have Pleasure in them, nor conceive by them. And, according to the Greatness or Smallness of this Part, they are more or less fond of Mens Embraces; so that it may properly be stil'd the Seat of Lust.

> Blowing the Coals up of those amorous Fires,
> Which Youth and Beauty to be quench'd requires.

And well may it be stil'd so; for it is like a Yard in Situation, Sub-stance, Composition and Erection. . . .

> Thus the Womens Secrets I have survey'd,
> And let them see how curiously they're made:
> And that, tho' they of different Sexes be,
> Yet in the whole they are the same as we:
> For those that have the strictest Searchers been,
> Find Women are but Men turn'd Out side in:
> And Men, if they but cast their Eyes about,
> May find they're Women, with their Inside out. . . .

Tho' there are some that desire not to have Children, and yet are very fond of nocturnal Embraces, to these Directions will be no way acceptable, because it may probably produce those Effects which they had rather be without; yet I doubt not, but that the Generality of both Sexes, when in a married State, hath such a Desire to produce the fair Image of themselves, that nothing can be more welcome to them, than those Directions that may make their mutual Embraces most effectual to that End: And therefore let none think it strange that we pretend to give Directions for the promoting of that which Nature itself teacheth all to perform. . . .

S. 3. A Word of Advice to both Sexes; or Directions respecting the Act of Coition, or carnal Copulation.

For the First, when married Persons design to follow the Propensions of Nature for the Production of the fair Images of themselves, let every Thing that looks like Care and Business be banish'd from their thoughts; for all such Things are Enemies to *Venus;* and let their animal and vital Spirits be powerfully exhilerated by some brisk and generous Restoratives; and let 'em to invigorate their Fancies, survey the lovely Beauties of each other, and bear the bright Idea's of them in their Minds; and if it happens, that instead of Beauty there is any Thing that looks like Imperfection or Deformity, (for Nature is not alike bountiful to all) let them be covered over with a Vail of Darkness, and buried in Oblivion. And since the utmost Intention of Desire is requir'd in this Act, it may not be amiss for the Bridegroom, for the more eager height'ning of his Joy, to delineate the Scene of their approaching Happiness to his fair languishing Bride, in some such amorous Raptures as this;

> Now my fair Bride, now will I storm the Mint
> Of Love and Joy, and rifle all that's in't.
> Now my infranchis'd Hand on every Side,
> Shall o'er thy naked polish'd Iv'ry slide:
> Freely shall now my longing Eyes behold
> Thy bared Snow, and thy unbraided Gold.
> Nor curtains now, tho' of transparent Lawn,
> Shall be before thy Virgin Treasure drawn:
> I will enjoy the now, my Fairest; come,
> And fly with me to Love's *Elizium:*
> My Rudder, with thy bold Hand, like a try'd
> And skilful Pilot, thou shalt steer; and guide
> My Bark in Love's dark Channel, where it shall

Dance, as the bounding Waves do rise and fall;
Whilst my tall Pinnace in the *Cyprian Strait,*
Ride safe at Anchor, and unlades the Freight.

Having by these, and other amorous Acts, (which Love can better dictate than my Pen) wound up your Fancies to the highest Ardour and Desires.

Perform those Rites Nature and Love requires,
'Till you have quench'd each others am'rous Fires.

And now for the Second Thing propos'd: When the Act of Coition is over, and the Bridegroom has done what Nature has prompted him too, he ought to take heed of withdrawing too suddenly out of the Field of Love, lest he should, by so doing, make way for Cold to strike into the Womb, which might be of dangerous Consequence: But when he has given Time for the Matrix to close up, which it naturally does soon after it has receiv'd the active Principle, in order to make a Conception; he may safely withdraw, and leave the Bride upon her soft Repose. . . . Neither should they too often reiterate those amorous Engagements, till the Conception be confirm'd: And even then the Bridegroom should remember, that 'tis a Market that lasts all the Year, and to be careful that he does not spend his Stock too lavishly: Nor will his Wife like him at all the worse for't: for generally women rather chuse to have a Thing done well, than have It often: And in this Case, to do it well and often too is inconsistent. But so much shall suffice for this.

After the Means made use of in order to Conception, according to the Directions before given there is Reason to expect that Coition should follow: But because the Success of all our Actions depends upon the Divine Blessing, and that Things do not always succeed according to our Desires, therefore Conception does not always follow upon Coition: For which Reason it is that many Women, especially those that are but newly married, know not whether they have conceiv'd or not, after Coition; which, if they were assur'd of they might and would avoid, several Inconveniences which they now run upon thro' Ignorance thereof. For, when after Conception a woman finds an Alteration in herself, and yet knows not from whence it arises, she is apt to run to a Doctor, and enquire of him what the Matter is, who, not knowing

S. 4. How a Woman may know whether she has conceiv'd.

that she is with Child, gives her perhaps a strong enthartical Potion, which certainly destroys the Conception.[4] There are others, that out of a foolish bashful Coyness, tho' they do know they have conceiv'd, yet will not confess it, that they may be instructed how to order themselves accordingly. Those that are coy may in Time learn to be wiser: And, for the Sake of those that are ignorant, I shall set down the Signs of Conception, that Women may thereby know, whether they have conceiv'd or not.

If a Woman hath conceiv'd, the Vein under the Eye will be swell'd. . . .

Again, stop the Urine of the Woman close in a Glass three Days, and then strain it through a fine Linen Cloth; if you find small living Creatures in it, she is most assuredly conceiv'd with Child. . . .

Also a Coldness and Chilness of the outward Parts after Copulation, shews a Woman to have conceiv'd, the Heat being retir'd to make the Conception: And then the Veins of the Breasts are more clearly seen than they were wont to be. The Tops of the Nipples look redder than formerly; the Body is weaken'd, and the Face discolour'd; the Belly waxeth very fat, because the Womb closeth itself together to nourish and cherish the Seed. If she drinks cold Water, a Coldness is felt in the Breasts; she has also Loss of Appetite, four Belchings, and exceeding Weakness of Stomach: The Breasts begin to swell, and wax hard, not without Pain or Soreness; wringing or grinding Pains like the Cramp happens in the Belly above the Navel: Also diverse Appetites and Longings are engender'd.[5] . . .

---

[4]The text is referring to the belief that regular menstruation kept the humors of the body in balance and was important to women's health; thus an "Alteration" or cessation of menses posed danger. This discussion is understood by historians to be an indirect reference intended to inform women that they might go to their physicians for medications to cause abortion.

[5]Produced.

The Second Framework:
Evangelical Christianity

2

LYMAN BEECHER

From *A Reformation of Morals Practicable and Indispensable*

1812

and

From *Resources of the Adversary and Means of Their Destruction*

1827

Lyman Beecher (1775–1863), the author of these sermons, was a key spokesman for the second framework, evangelical Christianity. A Presbyterian minister educated at Yale, he became a leader of the religious revival known as the Second Great Awakening. Remembered today as the father of Catharine Beecher, Harriet Beecher Stowe, and Henry Ward Beecher, he was a formidable figure in his own time. Lyman Beecher fostered religious and moral reform societies to usher in the Kingdom of God. He imagined the body as the battleground in the conflict between the soul implanted by God and the desires tempted by Satan.

Lyman Beecher, "A Reformation of Morals Practicable and Indispensable," 1812, and "Resources of the Adversary and Means of Their Destruction," 1827, from *Sermons Delivered on Various Occasions* (Boston: T. R. Marvin, 1828).

A Reformation of Morals Practicable and Indispensable

... From various causes the ancient discipline of the family has been extensively neglected. Children have neither been instructed in religion, nor governed in early life, as they were in the days of our fathers. The imported discovery, that human nature is too good to be made better by discipline, that children are enticed from the right way by religious instruction, and driven from it by the rod, and kept in thraldom by the conspiracy of priests and legislators, has united not a few in the noble experiment of emancipating the world, by the help of an irreligious, ungoverned progeny.

The indolent have rejoiced in the discovery, that our fathers were fools and bigots, and have cheerfully let loose their children, to help on the glorious work: While thousands of families having heard from their teachers or believing in spite of them, that morality will suffice, both for earth and heaven, and not doubting that morality will flourish without religion, have either not reared the family altar, or have put out the sacred fire and laid aside together the rod and the Bible, as superfluous auxiliaries in the education of children. From the school too, with pious regard for its sacred honours, the Bible has been withdrawn, lest by a too familiar knowledge of its contents, children should learn to despise it. As if ignorance were the mother of devotion, and the efficacy of laws depended upon their not being understood. With similar benign wisdom has not only the rod, but government and catechetical[6] instruction, and a regard to the moral conduct of children been exiled from the school. . . .

Much may be done in the way of prevention: but, in a free government, moral suasion[7] and coercion must be united. If children be not religiously educated and accustomed in early life to subordination, the laws will fail, in the unequal contest, of subduing tigers to their yoke. But if the influence of education and habit be not confirmed, and guarded by the supervening influence of law, this salutary restraint will be burst and swept away by the overpowering force of human depravity. To retrieve therefore our declension,[8] it is indispensable that new fidelity pervade not only the family, the school, and the church of

---

[6]The term *catechetical* relates to the catechism, or instruction, in the elementary principles of Christianity, usually by questions and answers.

[7]A version of the word "persuasion."

[8]*Declension* denotes the decline from a standard, here a moral one.

God, but that the laws against immorality be restored to their ancient vigour. . . .

Our fathers were not fools; as far from it were they as modern philosophers are from wisdom. Their fundamental maxim was, that man is desperately wicked, and cannot be qualified for good membership in society without the influence of moral restraint. With great diligence, they availed themselves therefore of the laws and institutions of revelation, as embodying the most correct instruction, and the most powerful moral restraint. The word of God was daily read and his worship celebrated in the family and in the school, and children were trained up under the eye of Jehovah. In this great work, pastors, and churches, and magistrates cooperated. And what moral restraint could not accomplish was secured by parental authority and the coertion of the law. . . .

If we do give up our laws and institutions, our guilt and misery will be very great.

We shall become slaves, and slaves to the worst of masters. The profane and the profligate,[9] men of corrupt minds, and to every good work reprobate,[10] will be exalted to pollute us by their example, to distract us by their folly, and impoverish us by fraud and rapine.[11] Let loose from wholesome restraint, and taught to sin by the example of the great, a scene, most horrid to be conceived, but more dreadful to be experienced, will ensue. . . .

Resources of the Adversary and Means of Their Destruction

The Scriptures teach, that sin commenced its reign on earth under the auspices of a mighty fallen spirit; and that he, having seduced mankind from their allegiance to God, has been constantly employed to maintain his bad eminence over them. They also teach, that the Son of God has interposed to destroy the works of this spirit; and that he will accomplish the object: that the power of Satan shall be broken; and the whole world be restored to loyalty and the favor of heaven. . . .

I am aware, that with some, the doctrine of fallen angels is but an

---

[9]The *profligate* here are dissipated persons, or ones who have abandoned themselves to vice.

[10]Men who are *reprobate* to every good work are sinners.

[11]Plunder.

eastern allegory; and the idea of a conflict, between the creature and Creator, ridiculous and unworthy of the divine supremacy. I can only say, that if there be not an order of sinful intelligences above men, the Bible is one of the most deceptive books ever written. . . . It is a matter of fact before our eyes—a matter of experience too—that the carnal mind is enmity against God; and that God, in Christ, is reconciling the world to himself. . . .

A new and mighty effort is demanded to send light through the territories of darkness—to repress crime and perpetuate our civil and religious institutions. In our large cities, especially, is the increase of ignorance and licentiousness lamentable and ominous. Here wealth and temptation concentrate their power upon masses of mind, whose influence cannot fail to affect deeply the destiny of the nation. If they send out a vigorous current of healthful life-blood, the whole nation will feel the renovating influence: but if, with every pulsation, they send out iniquity and death, no power on earth can avert our doom.

A *moral* power is the only influence that can save our cities. . . . Until our cities shall thus be made to feel, in every part, the purifying power of the Gospel, the whole land will continue to send to them, as it has done, hecatombs of youthful victims, to be repaid by disappointed hopes and moral contamination. . . .

3

LYMAN BEECHER

The Perils of Atheism to the Nation

1830

As an early nineteenth-century Presbyterian, Lyman Beecher fought hard against Catholics. A believer in the Trinity of Father, Son, and Holy Spirit, he opposed the new creed of Unitarianism that denied the Trinity and freethinkers who upheld rationalism and questioned religious thinking. In this lecture, Beecher expressed his fear that freethinkers were

Lyman Beecher, "The Perils of Atheism to the Nation," 1830, from *Lectures on Political Atheism and Kindred Subjects* (Boston: John P. Jewett & Company, 1852).

bringing to the United States the horrors of the later phases of the French Revolution, known as the Terror.

All governments originate in the necessities of self-defence against the violent evil propensities of man. . . .

There never has been but one government professedly atheistic. The National Assembly of France, in the commencement of the revolution, appointed a committee to inquire and report whether there were a God: and the committee reported that there could be no liberty on earth while there was believed to be a God in heaven; and that there is no God, and that death is an eternal sleep. The Assembly adopted the report, abolished the Sabbath, burnt the Bible, instituted the decade, and ordained the worship of the goddess of liberty, in the person of a vile woman. But the consequences were too terrible to be endured; it converted the most polished nation of Europe into a nation of fiends and furies, and the theatre of voluptuous refinement into a stall of blood. . . . And yet, this dreadful experiment these men would repeat upon us. The entire corroborating action of the government of God, with all its satellite institutions, they would abolish, to let out upon society in wrath, without mixture and without measure, the impatient depravity of man.

The family—the foundation of the political edifice, the methodizer of the world's business, and the mainspring of its industry—they would demolish. . . . The family—that school of indelible early impression, and of unextinguished affection—that verdant spot in life's dreary waste, about which memory lingers—that centre of attraction, which holds back the heady and high-minded, and whose cords bring out of the vortex the shipwrecked mariner, after the last strand of every other cable is parted—these political Vandals would dismantle. The fire on its altars they would put out; the cold hand of death they would place on the warm beatings of its heart; to substitute the vagrancy of desire, the rage of lust, and the solitude, and disease, and desolation, which follow the footsteps of unregulated nature, exhausted by excess. . . .

4

FRANCES WRIGHT

Nashoba, Explanatory Notes, &c. Continued
February 6, 1828

Frances Wright (1795–1852) was a critical influence on the third framework, the popular science of the body. A Scottish heiress and writer, she spoke and wrote in America in the late 1820s and early 1830s. Outspoken and brave, she brought unusual frankness to her discussions of sexuality and race. Her important work in the United States included founding Nashoba, a utopian colony outside of Memphis, Tennessee, designed to allow slaves to work for their freedom. When word got out that members of the community were involved in sexual relations outside of marriage that crossed the color line, Wright wrote a defense that contrasted natural sexual relations to marriage and opposed the disgrace cast on unwed mothers. She asserted that sexual passion was a great force if rightly used. Opposing both public opinion and law, Wright insisted that the true regulator of sexual passion was a person's knowledge of its consequences, not law or custom.

... The Institution of Nashoba being thus founded on the broad basis of human liberty and equality, every provision made by the legal act of the founder, as well as the subsequent regulations of the trustees are shaped in accordance with it.... Without disputing the established laws of the country, the institution recognizes *only within its bosom* the force of its own principles.

Frances Wright, "Nashoba, Explanatory Notes, &c. Continued," *New-Harmony Gazette*, No. 17, Feb. 6, 1828.

It is declared in the deed of the founder, that no individual can be received as member, but after a novitiate of six months, and then only by a *unanimous* vote of the resident proprietors. It is also provided that the admission of a husband shall not involve that of a wife, nor the admission of a wife that of a husband, nor the admission of either or both of the parents that of the children *above the age of fourteen*. . . . The marriage law existing without the pale of the Institution, is of no force within that pale. No woman can forfeit her individual rights or independent existence, and no man assert over her any rights or power whatsoever, beyond what he may exercise over her free and voluntary affections; nor, on the other hand, may any woman assert claims to the society or peculiar protection of any individual of the other sex, beyond what mutual inclination dictates and sanctions, while to every individual member of either sex is secured the protection and friendly aid of all.

The tyranny usurped by the matrimonial law over the most sacred of the human affections, can perhaps only be equalled by that of the unjust public opinion, which so frequently stamps with infamy, or condemns to martyrdom the best-grounded and most generous attachments, which ever did honor to the human heart, simply because unlegalized by human ceremonies, equally idle and offensive in the form and mischievous in the tendency.

This tyranny, as now exercised over the strongest and at the same time, if refined by mental cultivation, the noblest of the human passions, had probably its source in religious prejudice, or priestly rapacity, while it has found its plausible and more philosophical apology in the apparent dependence of children on the union of the parents. To this plea it might, perhaps, be replied, that the end, how important soever, is not secured by the means. That the forcible union of unsuitable and unsuited parents can little promote the happiness of the offspring; and supposing the protection of the children to be the real source and object of our code of morals and of our matrimonial laws, what shall we say of the effects of these humane provisions on the fate and fortunes of one large family of helpless innocents, born into the world in spite of all prohibitions and persecutions, and whom a cruel law, and yet more cruel opinion, disown and stigmatize. But how wide a field does this topic embrace! How much cruelty—how much oppression of the weak and the helpless does it not involve! The children denominated illegitimate, or *natural,* (as if in contradiction of others who should be *out of nature,* because *under law*) may be multiplied to any number by an unprincipled father, easily exonerated by law and custom from the duties of paternity, while these duties, and their accompanying shame, are left to a mother but too often rendered desperate by misfortune! And should we follow out our review of the law of civilized countries, we shall find the offspring termed legitimate, with whom honor and power and possession are associated, adjudged, in case of matrimonial dissensions to the father, who by means of this legal claim, has, not unfrequently, bowed to servitude the spirit of a fond mother, and held her, as a galley slave, to the oar. . . .

The writer of this article will, however, challenge all the advocates of existing institutions and existing opinions to test them by the secret feelings of their own bosoms, and then to pronounce on their justice. She will challenge them to consider the wide field of human society as now existing, to examine its practice and to weigh its theory, and to pronounce on the consistency of the one and the virtue of the other. She will challenge them to determine how many of the moral evils and numerous family of physical diseases, which now torture the human species, have not their source in the false opinion and vicious institutions which have perverted the best source of human happiness—the intercourse of the sexes—into the deepest source of human misery. Let us look into our streets, our hospitals, our asylums; let us look into the secret thoughts of the anxious parent trembling for the minds and bodies of sons starting into life, or mourning over the dying health of daughters condemned to the unnatural repression of feelings and desires inherent in their very organization and necessary alike to their moral and physical well-being. Or let us look to the victims—not of pleasure, not of love, nor yet of their own depravity, but of those ignorant laws, ignorant prejudices, ignorant code of morals, which condemn one portion of the female sex to vicious excess, another to as vicious restraint, and all to defenseless helplessness and slavery, and generally the whole of the male sex to debasing licentiousness, if not to loathsome brutality. . . .

In the moral, intellectual and physical cultivation of both sexes should we seek, as we can only find, the source and security of human happiness and human virtue. Prejudice and fear are weak barriers against passions, which, inherent in our nature and demanding only judicious training to form the ornament, and supply the best joys of our existence, are maddened into violence by pernicious example and pernicious restraint, varied with as pernicious indulgence. Let us correct our views of right and wrong, correct our moral lessons, and so correct the practice of rising generations! Let us not teach that virtue consists in the crucifying of the affections and appetites, but in their judicious government. Let us not attach ideas of purity to monastic chastity, impossible to man or woman without consequences fraught with evil, nor ideas of vice to connections formed under the auspices of kind feelings. Let us enquire, not if a mother be a wife, or a father a husband, but if parents can supply to the creatures they have brought into being, all things requisite to render existence a blessing! Let the force of public opinion be brought against the thoughtless ignorance, or cruel selfishness, which, either with or without the sanction of a legal or religious permit, so frequently multiplies offspring beyond the resources of the parents. Let us check the force of passions, as well as their precocity, not by the idle terror of imaginary crime in the desire itself, but by the just and benevolent apprehension of bringing into existence, unhappy or imperfect beings. Let us teach the young mind to reason, and the young heart to feel, and instead of shrouding our bodies, wants, desires, senses, affections and faculties in mystery, let us court enquiry, and show that acquaintance with our own nature can alone guide us to judicious practice, and that in the consequence of human actions, exists only the true test of their virtue or their vice.

5

FRANCES WRIGHT

On the Nature of Knowledge

1829

With Nashoba's failure, Wright moved to Indiana to join Robert Dale Owen in editing the New-Harmony Gazette *and became a lecturer. In 1829, she settled in New York, created the Hall of Science, published the* Free Enquirer, *and worked for public education and workers' rights. In this written version of one of her lectures, Frances Wright stated her belief that the only guide to truth was experience crystallized into science.*

Frances Wright, "On the Nature of Knowledge," *Course of Popular Lectures, as Delivered by Frances Wright, in New-York, Philadelphia, Baltimore, Boston, Cincinnati, St. Louis, Louisville, and Other Cities, Towns, and Districts of the United States* (New York: Office of the Free Enquirer, 1829).

. . . Sons and daughters of America! . . . When will ye improve the liberty for which your fathers sought an unknown world? When will ye appreciate the treasure they have won? When will ye see, that liberty leans her right arm on knowledge, and that knowledge points you to the world ye inhabit?

Consider that world, my friends! Enable yourselves, by mastering the first elements of knowledge, to judge of the nature and importance of all its different branches. Fit yourselves for the examination of your opinions, and then *examine your opinions.* Read, enquire, reason, reflect! Wrong not your understandings by doubting their perception of moral, any more than of physical, truth. Wrong not the God ye worship by imagining him armed with thunders to protect the tree of knowledge from approach. If ye conceive yourselves as holding from one great being your animate existence, employ his first best gift— your reason. Scan with your reason that which ye are told is his word, scan with your senses those which ye are told are his works. Receive no man's assertion. Believe no conviction but your own; and *respect not your own* until ye *know* that ye have examined both sides of every question; collected all evidence, weighed, compared, and digested it; sought it at the fountain head; received it never through auspicious channels—altered, mutilated, or defaced; but pure, genuine, from the authorities themselves. Examine ye things? look to the fact. Examine ye books? to the text. And, when ye look, and when ye read, be *sure that ye see, and be sure that ye understand.* Ask *why* of every teacher. Ask *why* over every book. While there is a doubt, suspend judgement; while one evidence is wanting, withhold assent.

Observe here the advantage of material science. Does the physician— (I use the word here, as I shall often have occasion to use it hereafter, to signify the student of physics, or the observer of nature)—does the physician tell you that water is compounded of gases? He performs the experiment. That the atmosphere is another compound? The same. That more or less of activity is in all matter? He shows you the formation of crystals in their bed, and composes and decomposes them before ye. Does he tell you that matter is ever changing, but never losing? He analyzes the substance before your eyes, and gives you its elements with nothing wanting. Do the anatomist and physiologist describe the structure and texture of your bodies? They show you their hidden arcana,[12] dissect their parts, and trace their relation; explain the mechanism of each organ, and observe,

[12]The secrets of nature.

with you, its uses and functions. Do the geologist and mineralogist speak to us of the structure and component parts of this globe? They explain to us the strata of earths; the position of rocks; the animal remains they envelope; the marks they exhibit of convulsion or of rest—of violent and sudden, or of gradual and silent, phenomena. See, then, the superiority of physical science! . . .

But, you will say, there is other evidence than the physically tangible—other truths than those admitted through the senses. There is the more *immediate* and the more *remote* testimony of our senses; nothing more, nothing less. Will you appeal to numerical and geometrical truth? Had we no senses, could we know any thing of either? Were there no objects, no substances and existences around you, how could you conceive of number or of form? If the child see not *four things,* how shall he understand the meaning of *four*? If he see not two halves, put them together, divide them, compare them, measure, weigh them, how shall he *know* that two halves are equal to a whole? or a whole greater than its part? These are the simple truths conceived by the philosopher of nature, Pestalozzi. Here are the leading beauties of that system of experimental instruction which he so long strove to put in practice, and which time may enable others successfully to develope.

But, I hear you again object, that there are truths appealing only to the mind, or directly to the feelings: such are *moral truths.* The varying degree of sensibility evinced by individuals towards the joys and sorrows of others is apparent to every observer. This sensibility forms the basis of virtue; and, when by means of experience we have distinguished painful from pleasurable sensations in our own case, this sensibility assists us to estimate them in the case of others. Yet have we no doors by which to admit knowledge but the senses. We ascertain what is good or evil by experience. The beneficial or injurious consequences of actions make us pronounce them virtuous or vicious. The man of cultivated sensibility then refers his sensations and applies his experience to others, and sympathises in the pain or the pleasure he conceives them to feel. But, here are our moral truths also based upon fact. There is no test of these but experience. That is good which produces good; that evil, which produces evil; and, were our senses different from what they are, our virtue and our vice would be different also. Let us have done with abstractions! Truth is fact. Virtue is beneficial action; vice, mischievous action; virtuous feelings are those which impart pleasure to the bosom; bad feelings, those which disturb and torment it. Be not anxious in seeking your rule of life. Consult experience; your own sensations, the sensations of others. These are surer guides than laws and doctrines, and when the law and the doctrines coincide not with the evidence of your senses, and the testimony of your reason, be satisfied that *they*, that is, the *law* and the *doctrine,* are false.

Think of these things! Weigh the truth of what I advance! Go to your churches with your understandings open. Enquire the meaning of the words ye hear—the value of the ideas. See if they be worth twenty millions of dollars! And, if they be not, withhold your contributions. But—ye will be afraid. Afraid! of what?—of acting conscientiously? of acting reasonably? Come! learn, then, of a stranger and a woman! Be bold to speak what ye think and feel; and to act in accordance with your belief. Prefer your self respect to the respect of others. Nay! *secure* your own respect, and *command* that of others. . . .

6

ROBERT DALE OWEN

From *Moral Physiology*

1831

Robert Dale Owen (1801–1877) initiated the third framework for the public deliberation of sex with Moral Physiology, *published in 1831, the first American work offering arguments for contraception. The son of Scottish industrialist and reformer Robert Owen, he came to the United States in 1825 as a young man to run his father's utopian community in New Harmony, Indiana, and edit the* New-Harmony Gazette. *In the late 1820s, he moved to New York where he co-edited the* Free Enquirer *with Frances Wright. In* Moral Physiology, *Owen presented favorably the contraceptive method of* coitus interruptus. *Although he discussed the condom, he judged it (in prevulcanized rubber days) both expensive and potentially unclean. As he anticipated the argument that any effort to interfere with conception is unnatural, he answered that, as with other*

Robert Dale Owen, *Moral Physiology; or, a Brief and Plain Treatise on the Population Question* (New York: Wright and Owen, 1831).

impulses, nature gave to humans both sexual desire and the capacity to control desire's effects.

Statement of the Subject

Among the human instincts which contribute to man's preservation and well-being, the instinct of reproduction holds a distinguished rank. It peoples the earth; it perpetuates the species. Controlled by reason and chastened by good feeling, it gives to social intercourse much of its charm and zest. Directed by selfishness, or governed by force, it is prolific of misery and degradation. Whether wisely or unwisely directed, its influence is that of a master principle, that colours, brightly or darkly, much of the destiny of man.

It is sometimes spoken of as a low and selfish propensity; and the Shakers call it a "carnal and sensual passion." I see nothing in the instinct itself that merits such epithets. Like other instincts, it may assume a selfish, mercenary, or brutal character. But, in itself, it appears to me the most social and least selfish of all our instincts. It fits us to give, even while receiving, pleasure; and, among cultivated beings, the former power is ever more highly valued than the latter. Not one of our instincts, perhaps, affords larger scope for the exercise of disinterestedness, or fitter play for the best moral feelings of our race. Not one gives birth to relations more gentle, more humanizing and endearing; not one lies more immediately at the root of the kindliest charities and most generous impulses that honour and bless human nature. Its very power, indeed, gives fatal force to its aberrations; even as the waters of the calmest river, when dammed up or forced from their bed, flood and ruin the country: but the gentle flow and fertilizing influence of the stream are the fit emblems of the instinct, when suffered, undisturbed by force or passion, to follow its own quiet channel.

That such an instinct should be thought and spoken of as a low, selfish propensity, and, as such, that the discussion of its nature and consequences should be almost interdicted in what is called decent society, is to me a proof of the profligacy of the age, and the impurity of the pseudo-civilized mind. I imagine that if all men and women were gluttons and drunkards, they would, in like manner, be ashamed to speak of diet or of temperance. . . .

. . . It sometimes happens, nay, it happens every day and hour, that mankind obey its impulses, not from any calculation of consequences, but simply from animal impulse. Thus many children that are brought into the world owe their existence, not to deliberate conviction in their parents that their birth was really desirable, but simply to an unreasoning instinct, which men, in the mass, have not learnt either to resist or control.

It is a serious question—and surely an exceedingly proper and important one—whether man can obtain, and whether he is benefitted by obtaining, control over this instinct. IS IT DESIRABLE, THAT IT SHOULD NEVER BE GRATIFIED WITHOUT AN INCREASE TO POPULATION? OR, IS IT DESIRABLE, THAT, IN GRATIFYING IT, MAN SHALL BE ABLE TO SAY WHETHER OFFSPRING SHALL BE THE RESULT OR NOT?

To answer the questions satisfactorily, it would be necessary to substantiate, that such control may be obtained without the slightest injury to the physical health, or violence to the moral feelings; and also, that it should be obtained without any real sacrifice of enjoyment; or, if that cannot be, with as little as possible. . . .

The Question Considered in Its Social Bearings

This is by far the most important branch of the question. The evils caused by an overstocking of the world, however inevitable, and distant; and an abstract view of the subject, if even unanswerable, does not come home to the mind with the force of detailed reality.

What would be the probable effect, in social life, if mankind obtained and exercised a control over the instinct of reproduction?

My settled conviction is—and I am prepared to defend it—that the effect would be salutary, moral, civilizing; that it would prevent many crimes and more unhappiness; that it would lessen intemperance and profligacy; that it would polish the manners and improve the moral feelings; that it would relieve the burden of the poor; and the cares of the rich; that it would most essentially benefit the rising generation, by enabling parents generally more carefully to educate, and more comfortably to provide for, their offspring. I proceed to substantiate as I may these positions.

And first, let us look solely to the situation of married persons. Is it not notorious, that the families of the married often increase beyond what a regard for the young beings coming into the world, or the happiness of those who give them birth, would dictate? In how many instances does the hard-working father, and more especially the mother, of a poor family, remain slaves throughout their lives, tugging at the oar of incessant labour, toiling to live, and living only to die;

when, if their offspring had been limited to two or three only, they might have enjoyed comfort and comparative affluence! How often is the health of the mother, giving birth every year to an infant—happy, if it be not twins—and compelled to toil on, even at those times when nature imperiously calls for some relief from daily drudgery—how often is the mother's comfort, health, nay, her life, thus sacrificed! . . .

With such a world as this, it is a difficult matter to reason. After listening to all I have said, it may perhaps cut me short by reminding me, that nature herself declares it to be right and proper, that we should reproduce our species without calculation or restraint. I will ask, in reply, whether nature also declares it to be right and proper, that, when the thermometer is at 96, we should drink greedily of cold water, and drop down dead in the streets? Let the world be told, that if nature gave us our passions and propensities, she gave us also the power wisely to control them; and that, when we hesitate to exercise that power, we descend to a level with the brute creation, and become the sport of fortune—the mere slaves of circumstance. . . .

However various and contradictory the different theories of generation, almost all physiologists are agreed, that the entrance of the sperm itself (or of some volatile particles proceeding from it) into the uterus, must precede conception. This it was that probably first suggested the possibility of preventing conception at will.

Among the modes of preventing conception which may have prevailed in various countries, that which has been adopted, and is now universally practised, by the cultivated classes on the continent of Europe, by the French, the Italians, and, I believe, by the Germans and Spaniards, consists of complete withdrawal, on the part of the man, immediately previous to emission. *This is, in all cases, effectual.* It may be objected, that the practice requires a mental effort and a partial sacrifice. I reply, that, in France, where men consider this, (as it ought ever to be considered, when the interests of the other sex require it,) a *point of honour*—*all* young men learn to make the necessary effort; and custom renders it easy and a matter of course. As for the sacrifice, shall a trifling (and it is but a very trifling) diminution of physical enjoyment be suffered to outweigh the most important considerations connected with the permanent welfare of those who are the nearest and dearest to us? . . . A cultivated young Frenchman, instructed as he is, even from his infancy, carefully to consult, on all occasions, the wishes, and punctiliously to care for the comfort and welfare, of the gentler sex, would learn almost with incredulity, that, in other countries, there are men to be found, pretending to cultivation,

who were less scrupulously honourable on this point than himself.
You could not offer him a greater insult than to presuppose the possibility of his forgetting himself so far, as thus to put his own momen-
tary gratification, for an instant, in competition with the wish or the
well-being of any one to whom he professed regard or affection. . . .

The least injurious among the present checks to population,
celibacy, is a mortification of the affections, a violence done to the
social feelings, sometimes a sacrifice even of the health. Not one of
these objections can be urged to the trifling restraint proposed. . . .

As to the practical efficacy of this simple preventative, the experience of France, where it is universally practised, might suffice in
proof. I know, at this moment, several married persons who have told
me, that, after having had as many children as they thought prudent,
they had for years employed this check, with perfect success. . . .

It may be said, and said truly, that this check places the power
chiefly in the hands of the man, and not, where it ought to be, in those
of the woman. She, who is the sufferer, is not secured against the cul-
pable carelessness, or perhaps the deliberate selfishness, of him who
goes free and unblamed, whatever may happen. To this, the reply is,
that the best and only effectual defence for women is to refuse connexion with any man *void of honour.* An (almost omnipotent) public
opinion would thus be speedily formed; one of immense moral utility,
by means of which the man's social reputation would be placed, as it
should be, in the keeping of women, whose moral tact and nice discrimination in such matters is far superiour to ours. How mighty and
how beneficent the power which such an influence might exert, and
how essentially and rapidly it might conduce to the gradual, but thorough extirpation of those selfish vices, legal and illegal, which now
disgrace and brutify our species, it is difficult even to imagine. . . .

Concluding Remarks

That most practical of philosophers, [Benjamin] Franklin, interprets
chastity to mean, *the regulated and strictly temperate satisfaction, without injury to others, of those desires which are natural to all healthy
adult beings.* In this sense, chastity is the first of virtues, and one most
rarely practised, either by young men or by married persons, even
when the latter most scrupulously conform to the letter of the law.*

---

*My father, Robert Owen's definition of chastity is also an excellent one: "PROSTITU-
TION, Sexual intercourse *without* affection; CHASTITY, Sexual intercourse *with* affection."

The promotion of such chastity is the chief object of the present work. It is all-important for the welfare of our race, that the reproductive instinct should never be selfishly indulged; never gratified at the expense of the well-being of our companions. A man who, in this matter, will not consult, with scrupulous deference, the slightest wishes of the other sex; a man who will ever put his desires in competition with theirs, and who will prize more highly the pleasure he receives than that he may be capable of bestowing—such a man appears to me, in the essentials of character, a brute. The brutes commonly seek the satisfaction of their propensities with straight-forward selfishness, and never calculate whether their companions are gratified or teased by their importunities. Man cannot assimilate his nature more closely to theirs, than by imitating them in this.

Again. There is no instinct in regard to which strict temperance is more essential. All our animal desires have hitherto occupied an undue share of human thoughts; but none more generally than this. The imaginations of the young and the passions of the adult are inflamed by mystery or excited by restraint, and a full half of all the thoughts and intrigues of the world has a direct reference to this single instinct. . . .

. . . Do we wish to bring this instinct under easy government, and to assign it only its due rank among human sentiments? Then let us cultivate the intellect, let us exercise the body, let us usefully occupy the time, of every human being. What is it [that] gives to passion its sway, and to desires their empire, now? It is vacancy of mind; it is listlessness of body; it is idleness. A cultivated race are never sensual; a hardy race are seldom love-sick; an industrious race have no time to be sentimental. Develope the moral sentiments, and they will govern the physical instincts. Occupy the mind and body usefully, intellectually; and the propensities will obtain that care and time only which they merit. Upon any other principle we may doctor poor human nature for ever, and shall only prove ourselves empirics in the end. Mortifications, vestal[13] vows, mysteries, bolts and bars, prudish prejudices—these are all quack-medicines; and are only calculated to prostrate the strength and spirits, or to heighten the fever, of the patient. If we will dislodge error and passion from the mind, we must replace them by something better. . . .

---

[13] *Vestal* is a way of saying virginal, or without sexual experience.

7

CHARLES KNOWLTON

From *Fruits of Philosophy*

1832

Charles Knowlton (1800–1850), a philosophically minded physician in western Massachusetts, wrote Fruits of Philosophy, *the first book on contraception in America based on medical knowledge of human reproduction. Published in 1832, it fully initiated the third framework for the public deliberation of sex. It was rewritten and reissued many times during and after his life, and its views were widely disseminated. Knowlton discussed what came to be known as the "douche method," instructing women to use a female syringe, an implement for injecting fluid into the vagina, immediately after sexual relations. Women were to put into a solution one of several well-known household chemicals that would destroy sperm before one could fertilize the female ovum. Because women had been douching in this manner with these substances to treat various conditions of the uterus and vagina for some time, the process (though not the timing) was familiar, the ingredients were known to be safe, and the female syringe was cheaply available at an apothecary. Knowlton faced repeated prosecutions for obscenity in Massachusetts for selling his* Fruits of Philosophy *and served time in jail, but ultimately he established a successful medical practice in Ashfield, Massachusetts.*

Preface

BY THE PUBLISHER

It is a notorious fact that the families of the married often increase beyond what a regard for the young beings coming into existence, or the happiness of those who give them birth, would dictate; and philanthropists, of first rate moral character, in different parts of the world, have for years been endeavoring to obtain and disseminate a knowledge of means whereby men and women may refrain at will from

Charles Knowlton, *Fruits Of Philosophy; Or, The Private Companion Of Young Married People* (New York, 1832).

becoming parents, without even a partial sacrifice of the pleasure which attends the gratification of the reproductive instinct. But no satisfactory means of fulfilling *this* object were discovered, until the subject received the attention of a physician who had devoted years to the investigation of the most recondite phenomena of the human system, as well as to chemistry. The idea occurred to him of destroying the fecundating property of the sperm by *chemical* agents; and upon this principle he devised "checks," which reason alone would convince us must be effectual, and which have been proved to be so, by actual experience.

This work, besides conveying a knowledge of these and other checks, contains much useful and interesting information relating to the generative function. It is written in a plain, yet chaste style. The great utility of such a work as this, especially to the *poor,* is ample apology (if apology be needed) for its publication.

Philosophical Proem[14]

... Agreeable consciousness constitutes what we call happiness; and disagreeable consciousness constitutes misery. As sensations are a higher degree of consciousness than mere thoughts, it follows, that agreeable sensations constitute a more exquisite happiness than agreeable thoughts. This portion of happiness which consists in agreeable sensations is commonly called *pleasure.* No thoughts are agreeable except those which were originally excited by, or have been associated with agreeable sensations. Hence, if a person never had experienced any agreeable sensations, he could have no agreeable thoughts; and would, of course, be an entire stranger to happiness.

There are five species of sensations, seeing, hearing, smelling, tasting and feeling. There are many varieties of feeling — as the feeling of hunger, thirst, cold, hardness, etc. Many of these feelings are excited by agents that act upon the exterior of the body, such as solid substances of every kind, heat and various other chemical irritants. Other feelings owe their existence to states or conditions of internal organs. These latter feelings are called *passions.*

Those passions which owe their existence chiefly to the state of the brain, or to causes acting directly upon the brain, are called the moral passions. — They are grief, anger, love, etc. They consist of sentient actions which commence in the brain and extend to the nerves in the

---

[14]A *proem* is a short introduction.

region of the stomach, heart, etc. But when the cause of the internal feeling of passion is seated in some organ remote of the brain, as in the stomach, the genital organs, etc. the sentient action which constitutes the passion, commences in the nerves of such organ and extends to the brain; and the passion is called an *appetite, instinct,* or *desire.* Some of these passions are natural, as hunger, thirst, the reproductive instinct, the desire to urinate, etc. Others are gradually acquired by habit. A *hankering* for stimulants, as spirits, opium and tobacco, is one of these.

Such is the nature of things, that our most vivid and agreeable sensations cannot be excited under all circumstances, nor beyond a certain extent under any circumstances, without giving rise, in one way or another, to an amount of disagreeable consciousness or misery, exceeding the amount of agreeable consciousness which attends such ill-timed or excessive gratification. To excite agreeable sensations to a degree not exceeding this certain extent, is *temperance;* to excite them beyond this extent, is *intemperance;* not to excite them at all, is mortification or abstinence. This certain extent varies with different individuals, according to their several circumstances, so that what would be temperance in one person may be intemperance in another.

To be free from disagreeable consciousness is to be in a state, which, compared with a state of misery, is a happy state; yet absolute happiness does not consist in the absence of misery—if it do, rocks are happy. It consists, as before said, in agreeable consciousness. That which enables a person to excite or maintain agreeable consciousness, is not happiness; but the *idea* of having such means in one's possession is agreeable, and of course, is a portion of happiness. Health and wealth go far in enabling a person to excite and maintain agreeable consciousness.

That which gives rise to agreeable consciousness is *good,* and we desire it. If we use it intemperately such use is bad, but the thing itself is still good. Those acts (and intentions are acts of that part of man which intends) of human beings which tend to the promotion of happiness, are good; but they are also called *virtuous* to distinguish them from other things of the same tendency. There is nothing for the word *virtue* to signify but virtuous actions. Sin signifies nothing but sinful actions, and sinful, wicked, vicious, or bad actions are those which are productive of more misery than happiness.

When an individual gratifies any of his instincts in a *temperate* degree, he adds an item to the sum total of human happiness, and causes the amount of human happiness to exceed the amount of misery farther than if he had not enjoyed himself; therefore it is virtuous, or, to say the least, it is not vicious or sinful for him so to do. . . .

Man by nature is endowed with the talent of devising means to remedy or prevent the evils that are liable to arise from gratifying our appetites; and it is as much the duty of the physician to inform mankind of the means of preventing the evils that are liable to arise from gratifying the reproductive instinct, as it is to inform them how to keep clear of the gout or the dyspepsia.[15] Let not the cold ascetic say we ought not to gratify our appetites any farther than is necessary to maintain health and to perpetuate the species. Mankind will *not so* abstain, and if means to prevent the evils that may arise from a farther gratification can be devised, they *ought not.* Heaven has not only given us the capacity of greater enjoyment, but the talent of devising means to prevent the evils that are liable to arise therefrom; and it becomes us, "with thanksgiving," to make the most of them.

Chapter III. Some Other Things Which Ought to Be Known

. . . While the gratification of the reproductive instinct, under such circumstances, and in such manner as I have mentioned, leads to bad consequences, a temperate and natural gratification under proper circumstances is attended with good—besides the mere attendant pleasure, which alone is enough to recommend such gratification. I admit that human beings might be so constituted that if they had not reproductive instinct to gratify, they might enjoy good health; but being constituted as they are, this instinct cannot be mortified with impunity. It is a fact universally admitted, that unmarried females do not enjoy so much good health, and attain to so great an age as the married; not withstanding the latter are subject to the diseases and pains incident to childbearing. A temperate gratification promotes the secretions, and the appetite for food; calms the restless passions; induces pleasant sleep; awakens social feelings; and adds a zest to life which makes one conscious that life is worth preserving.

Chapter IV. Of the Checks

The *first* check I shall mention is one which has undoubtedly occurred to the minds of many. It consists in an *entire withdrawal* on the part of

---

[15]Disorder of the digestive system, especially the stomach.

the male, immediately previous to emission. A partial withdrawal is not to be depended on, since pregnancy has occurred even where the hymen remained entire. This Check, it is true, requires a slight mental effort and a partial sacrifice of enjoyment; but it is said, habit soon renders the effort of no account—and as to the slight sacrifice, a man of honor will not suffer it to outweigh a regard for the happiness of her whom he professes to love, nor to outweigh the risk of incurring heavy and sacred responsibilities, ere he is prepared to meet and fulfil them. . . .

A *second* Check consists in introducing into the vagina, previous to coition a fine soft sponge moistened with *chloride of soda** to be immediately afterwards withdrawn, by means of a very narrow ribbon attached to it. The sponge should be of a spherical shape; and in no case, probably, does the diameter of the piece ought to be less than one inch and three quarters, when moist and not compressed. With those who have had children, a larger piece, generally, will be required, than with others. If in any case the chloride should irritate (which irritation would be of a healthy kind and soon pass off,) it may be weakened with a little water until it do not irritate. It is a powerfully detergent article, and if used by *every* one, that foul disease[16] which probably originated in frequent promiscuous intercourse, and is propagated by contact, would doubtless soon become extinct.

The sponge moistened with *water,* has undoubtedly proven effectual in great proportion of cases in which it has been used, but It has occasionally failed; and this is what we should have expected, considering the viscidity of the semen, the anatomy of the parts. . . .

A *third* Check consists in the use, by the male, of a covering made of a very delicate skin. It is a sure preventive—but it is highly objectionable on the score of cleanliness and expense; a bandruche, as it is called, being fit for use but once, and costing about a dollar.

A *fourth* check with which I am acquainted, operates both mechanically and chemically, and will, I think, be generally preferred to either of the foregoing. It consists in syringing the vagina immediately after connexion, with a solution of sulphate of zinc, of alum, pearlash, or any salt that acts chemically on the semen, and at the same time pro-

---

*A bottle containing a pint and a half, or more, of the Chloride of Soda, may be had at the apothecary's for about four shillings. It is of uniform strength when purchased. The bottle should be kept corked.

[16]*That foul disease* is likely a reference to venereal disease, such as gonorrhea or syphilis.

duces no unfavorable effect on the female. In all probability, a vegetable astringent would answer — as an infusion of white oak bark, of red rose leaves. . . . A *female syringe,* which will be required in the use of this check, may be had at the shop of an apothecary, for a shilling or less. . . .

I know the use of this Check requires the woman to leave her bed for a few moments, but this is its only objection; and it would be unreasonable to suppose that any Check can ever be devised entirely free of objections. In its favor, it may be said, it costs nearly nothing — it is sure; it requires no sacrifice of pleasure; it is in the hands of the female; it is to be used *after,* instead of before connexion, a weighty consideration in its favor, as a moments reflection will convince anyone; and last but not least conducive to cleanliness, and preserves the parts from relaxation and disease. . . . Those who have used this Check (and some have used it to my certain knowledge, with entire success, for nine or ten years, and under such circumstances as leave no room to doubt its efficacy) affirm that they would be at the trouble of using injections merely for the purposes of health and cleanliness.

CHRISTIAN REFORM PHYSIOLOGY

8

SYLVESTER GRAHAM

On the Science of Human Life

1834

Sylvester Graham (1794–1851) contributed a powerful and influential Christian voice to the third framework for the public deliberation of sex. Originally intending to join the ministry as had his father and grandfather before him, he instead became a lecturer and a promoter of temperance. Studying the physiology of his day, he also became an advocate for diet reform. He accepted the distinction of two nervous systems that control bodily functions. He saw the reproductive function as unique in

Sylvester Graham, *A Lecture to Young Men* (Providence, R.I.: Weeden and Cory, 1834).

that it engaged both nervous systems: the nerves of organic life, attached to the stomach; and the nerves of animal life, tied to the brain. Because nutrition and the other vital functions of life depended on the nervous system, a man needed to be protected from the excitement of sexual intercourse; for this reason, Graham counseled sexual restraint in marriage.

So numerous, and universal, and continual are the evils which the human race have suffered in this world, that we are accustomed to consider disease and pain, as the necessary afflictions which legitimately grow out of our constitutional nature and appropriate circumstances: and hence we either bear these afflictions with what resignation we are capable of, as the wise dispensations of a good and merciful Creator, or sullenly and proudly endure them, with what fortitude we possess, as the blind and unavoidable casualties of inexorable fate. In both cases we are almost equally in error; and by our false notions, prevent those advantages which we might otherwise gain by our experience.

Be assured, my young friends, the human system is constructed entirely upon principles of benevolence; and perfectly adapted to an end of utility and enjoyment. Disease and suffering are in no degree, the legitimate and necessary results of the operations of our bodily organs; and by no means necessarily incident to human life. The constitutional nature of man, is established upon principles, which, when strictly obeyed, will always secure his highest good and happiness:— and every disease, and every suffering which human nature bears, result from the violation of the constitutional laws of our nature.

If mankind always lived precisely as they ought to live, they would—as a general rule—most certainly pass through the several stages of life, from infancy to extreme old age, without sickness and pain,—enjoying through their long-protracted years, health, and serenity, and peace, and individual, and social happiness; and gradually wear out their vital energies; and finally, lie down, and fall asleep in death, without an agony—without a pain. . . .

Whatever, therefore, increases your knowledge of your constitutional nature, and makes you better acquainted with those laws of life, upon which your health and happiness depend, cannot be otherwise than interesting to you.

Constituted as man is, two grand FUNCTIONS of his system, are necessary for his existence as an individual, and as a species.

The first is NUTRITION:—the second is REPRODUCTION.

Nutrition is the general function by which the body is nourished and sustained; and includes, in its detail, digestion, absorption, circulation, respiration, secretion, excretion &c. Reproduction is the function by which an organized being propagates its kind. The first is necessary for man's individual, bodily existence. The second is necessary for the continuation of his species.

Man is accordingly furnished with organs fitted for these great functions of life. . . .

But the function of reproduction is not necessary for man's individual existence, and therefore its final cause, or constitutional purpose, does not require its constant exercise: and accordingly, the organs, constituting the apparatus necessary for this function, are not all complete until many years after birth.

In the lower orders of animals, both of these important functions, are under the control of instinct; and therefore, the range of their exercise, is more strongly defined and limited. . . . But in man, these important functions—and especially that of reproduction—are, as to their exercise, placed under the control of his rational powers. . . .

Be it understood, however, that man, in a pure state of nature, would come under the government of instinct in regard to the function of reproduction, equally with the lower orders of animals;—that is,—he would have no disposition to exercise this function to any injurious excess, beyond the purposes of his organization. It is by abusing his organs, and depraving his instinctive appetites, through the devices of his rational powers, that the body of man, has become a living volcano of unclean propensities and passions. . . .

The functions of nutrition and reproduction depend on the vital properties of the tissues which form the organs of the system—particularly the muscular and nervous tissues; and more especially the nervous.

The nerves belonging to the human body, are divided into two classes.

First; the BRAIN and SPINAL MARROW, with their various cords, branches, fibres and filaments. These nerves appertain to what is called *Animal Life,* and are the organs of sensation, perception, intellection, volition; and are connected with the muscles of voluntary motion.

Second; the GANGLIONS and PLEXUSES with their various cords, branches, fibres and filaments. These nerves appertain to what is called *Organic Life.* They are distributed to the various internal organs, and preside over all the processes of vital chemistry. . . .

The genital organs are, as it were, woven into the same grand web of organic life, with the stomach, heart, lungs, &c. by being largely supplied from the same class of nerves on which the organs of nutrition depend for their functional power:—but the genital organs are also supplied with nerves of animal life, or those which are connected with the brain and spinal marrow. Hence the influences of the brain may act directly on the genital organs; and of these latter, on the brain. Lascivious thoughts and imaginations will excite and stimulate the genital organs; cause an increased quantity of blood to flow into them; and augment their secretions and peculiar sensibilities:—and, on the other hand, an excited state of the genital organs, either from the stimulations of semen, or from diseased action in the system, will throw its influence upon the brain, and force lascivious thoughts and imaginations upon the mind. . . .

The nerves appertaining to organic life, which preside over the general function of nutrition, are, in their natural and healthy state, entirely destitute of sensibility; and the perfect healthfulness and integrity of this general function, require such a state of these nerves. All extraordinary and undue excitements, however, whether caused by mental, moral or physical stimuli, increase the excitability and unhealthy activity of the nerves of organic life; and tend to induce diseased irritability and sensibility in them, which is more or less diffused over the whole domain; and affects all the particular organs and functions. A frequent repetition of these excitements, always induces a greater or less degree of debility and diseased irritability in the nerves of organic life;—disordering and deranging the functions, and often causing excessive morbid irritability and sensibility and inflammation, and even disorganization or change of structure in the viscera—such as the brain, stomach, lungs, liver, kidneys, heart, &c.

Thus the passions, such as anger, fear, grief, &c., when violent and frequent or continued, irritate and debilitate the nerves of organic life, and induce in them, a state of morbid irritability, and thereby disorder all the organic functions of the system, and lead to the most painful and often the most fatal diseases. The nerves of the genital organs partake, in common with those of the other organs, of this general debility and diseased excitability, and become exceedingly susceptible of irritation; sympathizing powerfully with all the disturbances of the system, and especially of the brain, and alimentary canal. Their peculiar sensibilities are augmented to a morbid or preternatural state, of a chronic character; and thus a diseased prurience,[17] or concupisence,[18] is permanently established,—forcing the sufferer into excessive desires, and unclean thoughts, almost incessantly. Hence hypochondriacs, and those who are afflicted with nervous melancholy, are generally morbidly lecherous; and hence, also, insanity, resulting from the morbid condition of the nerves of organic life, is generally attended with excessive sexual desire, and the mind becomes filled with unclean images. This is the reason why many people, who were perfectly modest while in health, become exceedingly obscene in their conduct and talk, when insane; and often, if they are not prevented, give themselves up to self-pollution, and thus exceedingly aggravate and confirm their disorders.

All kinds of stimulating and heating substances; high-seasoned food; rich dishes; the free use of flesh; and even the excess of aliment; all, more or less,—and some to a very great degree—increase the concupiscent excitability and sensibility of the genital organs, and augment their influence on the functions of organic life, and on the intellectual and moral faculties. . . .

The convulsive paroxysms attending venereal indulgence, are connected with the most intense excitement, and cause the most powerful agitation to the whole system, that it is ever subject to. The brain, stomach, heart, lungs, liver, skin—and the other organs—feel it sweeping over them, with the tremendous violence of a tornado. The powerfully excited and convulsed heart drives the blood, in fearful congestion, to the principal viscera,—producing oppression, irritation, debility, rupture, inflammation, and sometimes disorganization;—and this violent paroxysm is generally succeeded by great exhaustion, relaxation, lassitude, and even prostration.

These excesses, too frequently repeated, cannot fail to produce the most terrible effects. The nervous system, even to its most minute filamentary extremities, is tortured into a shocking state of debility, and excessive irritability, and uncontrolable mobility, and aching sensibility: and the vital contractility of the muscular tissues throughout the whole system, becomes exceedingly impaired, and the muscles generally, become relaxed and flaccid; and consequently, all the organs and vessels of the body, even to the smallest capillaries, become extremely debilitated; and their functional power, exceedingly feeble. . . .

[17] A craving.
[18] Lust or libidinous desire.

We are told by some writers on this important subject, that the genital secretion, or "the semen, may be called the essential oil of animal liquors—the rectified spirit—the most subtle and spirituous part of the animal frame, which contributes to the support of the nerves;—that the greatest part of this refined fluid is, in a healthy state and conduct of the system, re-absorbed and mixed with the blood, of which it constitutes the most rarified and volatile part, and imparts to the body, peculiar sprightliness, vivacity, muscular strength, and general vigor and energy to the animal machine;—that it causes the beard, hair and nails to grow,—gives depth of tone, and masculine scope and power to the voice,—and manliness and dignity to the countenance and person; and energy, and ardor, and noble daring to the mind: and therefore that the emission of semen, enfeebles the body more than the loss of twenty times the same quantity of blood,—more than violent cathartics[19] and emetics[20]:—and hence the frequent and excessive loss of it, cannot fail to produce the most extreme debility, and disorder, and wretchedness of both body and mind." . . .

Physiologists have indulged in a great deal of conjecture and speculation concerning the "animal spirits—nervous fluid—vital electricity," &c. &c., but as yet, it is all conjecture and speculation. We know that, by some means or other, the influence of the WILL, is conveyed through certain nerves, to the organs of voluntary motion—that the sense of touch is conveyed, or reflected, or transmitted from the surface, through certain other nerves, to the brain:—and that vital energy is distributed through certain other nerves, from the general and particular centres of action, to the several organs, for the supply of their functional powers:—and we know, too, that in the functional exercise of the genital organs, something very analogous to electricity or galvanism, diffuses a peculiar and powerful excitement, and sensation, throughout the whole nervous system. Now, whether these vital effects are produced by means of nervous fluid or spirit, or something still more subtle and intangible,—or by some other means; human research and investigation have not ascertained, and perhaps never will. But we are perfectly certain, that the peculiar *excitement* of venereal indulgence, is more diffusive, universal and powerful, than any other to which the sytem [*sic*] is ever subject; and that it more rapidly exhausts the vital properties of the tissues, and impairs the functional powers of the organs: and consequently, that it, in a greater degree

---

[19]Medicines used to purge or evacuate the bowels.
[20]Medicines used to induce vomiting.

than any other cause, deteriorates all the vital processes of nutrition, from beginning to end; and therefore, more injuriously affects the character and condition of all the fluids and solids of the body;—and hence the terrible fact, that venereal excesses occasion the most loathsome, and horrible, and calamitous diseases that human nature is capable of suffering. . . .

Hence, therefore, SEXUAL DESIRE, cherished by the mind and dwelt on by the imagination, not only increases the excitability and peculiar sensibility of the genital organs themselves, but always throws an influence, equal to the intensity of the affection, over the whole nervous domain;—disturbing all the functions depending on the nerves for vital energy, which is thereby increased upon, or distracted from them;—and, if this excitement is frequently repeated, or long continued, it inevitably induces an increased degree of irritability and debility, and relaxation generally throughout the nervous and muscular tissues, and especially the nerves of organic life. And, hence, those LASCIVIOUS DAY-DREAMS, and *amorous reveries,* in which young people too generally,—and especially the idle, and the voluptuous, and the sedentary, and the nervous,—are exceedingly apt to indulge, are often the sources of general debility, effeminacy, disordered functions, and permanent disease, and even premature death, without the actual exercise of the genital organs! Indeed! this unchastity of thought—this *adultery of the mind,* is the beginning of immeasurable evil to the human family:—and, while children are regularly trained to it, by all the mistaken fondness of parents, and all the circumstances of civic life, it is but mockery in the ear of Heaven, to deprecate the evil consequences; and folly, little short of fatuity,[21] to attempt to arrest the current of crime that flows from it. . . .

There is a common error of opinion among young men, which is, perhaps, not wholly confined to the young,—that health requires an emission of semen at stated periods, and that frequent nocturnal emissions in sleep, are not incompatible with health. All this is wrong,—entirely, dangerously wrong! . . .

[21] *Fatuity* means, in this context, idiocy or dementia.

9

SYLVESTER GRAHAM

On Self-Pollution

1834

During the antebellum years, masturbation became an obsessional concern for many writers about sexuality. It was Sylvester Graham who helped initiate the panic. He regarded youthful masturbation as particularly dangerous to health, posing special risks because of the immaturity of children's reproductive organs and because the play of imagination and the need of no second party led young people to frequent practice.

By far the worst form of venereal indulgence, is self-pollution; or, what is called "Onanism." . . .[22]

This exceedingly pernicious practice, I say, is incomparably the worst form of venereal indulgence: and for several important reasons.

In the first place, it is wholly unnatural; and, in every respect, does violence to nature. The mental action, and the power of the imagination on the genital organs, forcing a vital stimulation of the parts, which is reflected over the whole nervous system, are exceedingly intense and injurious; and consequently the reciprocal influences between the brain and genital organs become extremely powerful, and irresistible and destructive. . . .

In the second place, it is generally commenced very early in life. All who are acquainted with the science of human life, are well aware that all excesses, and injuries of every kind, are far more pernicious and permanent in their effects on the youthful and growing body, than

[22]Masturbation was called *Onanism* because it was associated with the sin of Judah's son Onan, who "spilled" his seed. (Genesis 38:9: "And Onan knew that the seed should not be his; and it came to pass, when he went in unto his brother's wife, that he spilled it on the ground, lest that he should give seed to his brother.")

Sylvester Graham, *A Lecture to Young Men* (Providence, R.I.: Weeden and Cory, 1834).

when all the organs and parts are completely developed, and the constitution and general economy, fully and firmly established. . . .

. . . Whatever may be the age of puberty—which in our country, rarely takes place in males earlier than about the fourteenth or fifteenth year of life—certain it is, that all venereal use of the genital organs, before that time, is shockingly unnatural and pernicious. Yet it is generally previous to this time, and frequently many years before it, that the debasing and ruinous practice of self-pollution is commenced. Indeed, the habit has in some instances been begun as early as the fifth or sixth year: and shocking as it may seem, nurses, and even *parents,* have been the teachers of this abominable vice! . . . Servants, and other laboring people of loose morals, often become the secret preceptors of children in this dreadful vice. It is, however, more frequently communicated from one boy to another; and sometimes a single boy will corrupt many others. But the most fruitful sources of instruction in this vice, are our public schools,[23]—and especially boarding-schools and colleges. The extent to which this evil prevails, and of the mischief resulting from it, in most of these institutions, is, perhaps, beyond credibility: and none but those who are instructed on this subject, can have any just apprehensions of the difficulties in preventing it. . . . The common notion that boys are generally ignorant in regard to this vice, and that we ought not to remove that ignorance, is wholly incorrect. I am confident that I speak within bounds, when I say, that seven out of every ten boys in this country, at the age of twelve, are, at least, acquainted with this debasing practice: and I say, again; the extent to which it prevails in our public schools and colleges, is shocking, beyond measure! . . .

In the third place; it is a secret and solitary vice, which requires the consent of no second person,—and therefore the practice has little to prevent its frequency: and as it necessarily and very soon produces a preternatural prurience in the genital organs, and a reciprocity of influence between these and the brain, which leads to the permanent establishment of those associations of the mind with the unclean sensibility, that, on all occasions of opportunity, suggest the deed,— the practice almost inevitably becomes more and more frequent, as the mischievous effects are experienced, until it sometimes reaches the most ruinous excess, and acquires a power which irresistibly urges on the unhappy sufferer, in the voluntary course of self-destruction. I

---

[23]By *public schools,* Graham did not mean tax-supported schools; rather, he meant education outside the household.

have had boys come to me, with complaints of ill health, who, on being closely questioned on this point, have confessed that they had indulged in this vice as often as three times in twenty-four hours; and sometimes thrice in a single night; and this, in some instances, years before the period of puberty. In fact, a very considerable proportion of the dyspepsia, and other forms of chronic disease, in our country, may be traced back to the early frequency of this vice, as one of their roots.

In the fourth place; it impairs the intellectual and moral faculties, and debases the mind, in the greatest degree; and causes the most deep and lasting regret, which sometimes rises to the most pungent remorse and despair. It would seem as if God had written an instinctive law of remonstrance, in the innate moral sense, against this filthy vice; for, however ignorant the boy may be, of the moral character of the act,—or of the physical and mental evils which result from it; though he may never have been told that it is wrong; yet every one who is guilty of it, feels an instinctive shame, and deep self-loathing, even in his secret solitude, after the unclean deed is done! and that youth has made no small progress in the depravity of his moral feelings, who has so silenced the dictates of natural modesty, that he can, without the blush of shame, pollute himself in the presence of another—even his most intimate companion! Hence, all who give themselves up to the excesses of this debasing vice, carry about with them, continually, a consciousness of their defilement, and cherish a secret suspicion that others look upon them as debased beings. . . .

10

LUTHER V. BELL, M.D.

From *An Hour's Conference with Fathers and Sons*
1840

Luther V. Bell (1806–1862) was one of many writers to sound the alarm against masturbation. A physician trained at Bowdoin College and Dartmouth Medical School, he helped found psychiatry in the United

Luther V. Bell, M.D., *An Hour's Conference with Fathers and Sons, in Relation to a Common and Fatal Indulgence of Youth* (Boston: Whipple and Damrell, 1840).

States. In 1837, he became medical superintendent of the McLean Asylum for the Insane near Boston, a position he held for the next two decades. An important element that Bell adds to consideration is his ungrounded assertion that masturbation was more common among leisured middle-class youth in school than among those forced to labor with their hands. In suggesting that laziness, an aversion to the opposite sex, and failures of boys to live up to contemporary notions of masculinity stem from masturbation, Bell alluded to a broader range of male adolescent behavior in his era than was usually considered in discussions in antebellum America.

Chapter I. General Want of Information on This Subject

It is a fact, curious and interesting, though perhaps somewhat humiliating to the pride of human intellect, that in these days of unrestrained investigation and ceaseless mental activity, there are frequently new discoveries of truth in relation to matters immediately before us, compelling us to an entire change in conclusions before deemed the most fixed, and presenting objects to our sight before unsuspected and unseen. . . .

In New England, within the last half dozen years, there have been circulated pretty extensively, the reports of the several institutions for the cure and custody of the insane. While casting an eye over these annual documents, many an intelligent and well-informed individual has probably noticed, for the first time in his life, the word *masturbation.* He remarks, amongst the various known *causes of insanity,* that this unknown word is more frequently repeated than even intemperance, ill health, loss of property, death of friends, or any other of the causes, moral or physical, in the melancholy catalogue of events preceding the overthrow of reason. The dictionary which he consults will probably give him no clue to its meaning. . . . When some friend, more inquisitive, intimates that it means nothing more nor less than the practice of imitating the act of sexual connection upon the individual's own person, perpetrated with his own hand, he will be lost in amazement and incredulity, that an act so commonly, I may say so universally, known amongst young men as this is, should be connected with insanity to such a frightful extent, and yet that he should now for the first time have an intimation of this fact. He is almost tempted to doubt, whether there is not some misapprehension or mistake, in that so strange a result exists, of which, if well-grounded and veritable, he certainly must have heard before this late day. . . .

Chapter II. Prevalence of the Evil

I have hinted my belief, that this act is almost universally known amongst the young men of New England. The reasons which induce me to think so are, that after more than a dozen years' experience in the practice of medicine, and this too particularly among the younger classes of the community; and during the last part of this period being compelled to scrutinize minutely into its existence as a cause of disease, I never yet have met with the young man, who has not at once apprehended (as his eye and countenance assured me) any indirect and distant allusion to it. And whether or not he admitted himself, in so many words, to be its victim, he acknowledged its existence in others, and comprehended the vulgar colloquial terms employed amongst lads in expressing the idea. My own observations have been corroborated by professional gentlemen of far wider experience than myself; and especially by one who, for over twenty years, followed his profession in the vicinity of one of our most frequented colleges.

I have spoken of the frightful ratio which this pernicious habit bears upon the registers of our principal asylums for lunatics, *among the causes of insanity.* . . . In the State Lunatic Hospital, at Worcester, Massachusetts, there were, during the last year (1838), one hundred and ninety-nine male patients; of these, by the superintendent's report, the alleged cause in forty-two was masturbation. At the McLean Asylum, near Boston, a department of the Massachusetts General Hospital, one hundred and twenty-eight males were in the institution, during the same year, of whom twenty-four owed their disease to the same cause; presenting the astounding fact that, of these three hundred and twenty-seven men, in the two principal hospitals of New England, sixty-six, or one-fifth of the whole number, owed their disease, not to the mysterious dispensations of Providence, in the loss of health, in the loss of property, in the death of friends, and the like, but to the voluntary indulgence of an unnatural, depraved, degrading, animal propensity! . . .

Chapter III. Predisposing Causes of the Habit

. . . Experience shows, that this is a true view of the subject; that a majority of its victims are among those whose fate it is not to be condemned to hard labor of the hands; but amongst the youth for whom fortune and circumstance seem to have done the most. The apprentice boy, whose master calls at earliest dawn to use the hammer or the saw, has little time, in the busy application of his working hours, to conjure up and dwell upon, until they almost assume the distinctness of real existences, the libidinous pictures of a foul imagination; at night, his weary frame sinks almost on reaching his hard mattress, into a slumber so deep and entire, that he has no temptation to spend the watches of the night in morbid contemplations and polluting dreams. Not so the pale student of the school, the college or the theological seminary; for, as we have had abundant reason for knowing, so little have our young men been awakened to the moral bearings of this vice, that no standing in the religious or moral world forms even a presumption against the probability of its existence, and should not for a moment divest the vigilance of the anxious parent, the conscientious friend, or the honest physician, when any circumstances lead to apprehension. The student, unawakened to a knowledge of the dire injury he is doing himself, retires to the solitude of his own chamber or study, or other place of privacy; no duties are so urgent as to make every moment of his time of consequence (of appreciable pecuniary value to another), and hence he may spend by himself, unsuspected and uninterfered with, hour after hour, and day after day, in contemplations, in studies, in pictures and day-dreams, administering and catering to this horrid appetite. Even the cultivation of his imagination and fancy, the end at least of a part of his education, may perhaps add to his power of depicting to himself imaginary scenes of voluptuous enjoyment and licentious opportunity, and which, like an unnatural stimulus, keeps up and rekindles the fires of amativeness,[24] when almost extinguished by the repetitions of this act.

I have been led to believe that a peculiar and intimate connection will be found to exist between the prevalence of this habit and the indulgence of an unrestrained pruriency of imagination. I have found, on being let into the inmost soul of many of these victims, on hearing the full, frank and detailed history of their painful career, its commencement and progress, that they almost universally have dwelt much upon their having cultivated and maintained the faculty of keeping constantly before them libidinous images, which they had taught their willing fancy to change, and color, and renew, as fast as they themselves were jaded by the repetition of imaginary enjoyments. I fear, that in our system of education of youth, due caution is not had in

---

[24]The arousal of feelings of sexual desire. The organ of amativeness was thought to be located at the base of the skull, the link between the brain and the spinal column. See the phrenological map (Figure 5).

training and restraining the imagination. Every library, public and private, every classic, every print-shop, has something, prose, poetry, or picture, which can be perverted,—if you choose so to consider what is a direct and natural result, a consequence following a cause,—to the base use of exciting the passions, and which is impressed into the service of pollution. Our whole literature, ancient and modern, if for no other reason than its natural tendency to administer to the depraved and vitiated tastes of our nature, demands expurgation. Many a man, whose eye is resting on these lines, will recall, while the blush of shame mantles on his burning cheek at the recollection, the volume, the page, the print to which he turned in ardent youth. . . .

I fear that the modern theatre has much to answer for in perverting and debasing the moral purity of our youth. Since the era of the importation of French dancing, will it be believed, that one of the most attractive and successful forms of theatrical amusement has consisted in the exhibition of what is virtually the nude female! . . .

After having thus given some idea of the extent to which this habit prevails, and among what classes its victims are, some elucidation will be made of the circumstances which give rise to it.

It is known by all, that at that period of life denominated puberty, in the healthy and matured subject, the propensity described as amativeness, by the phrenologists, naturally and spontaneously occupies no small space in the physical development, as well as the moral character of the individual. The young man feels within himself an aching void to be satisfied. The natural mode of gratification, at this period, would be alike inexpedient and impracticable, in a civilized state of society, involving in the very idea, such a state of morals as we have spoken of as existing in the most abandoned parts of the world. And in the unformed, immature condition of the physical system, at the date of the first evolution of the reproductive instinct, an unbridled indulgence could not fail to prove destructive to the perfection of the bodily powers, as well as to be highly detrimental to the moral and mental development.

Now this instinct, thus brought into activity, is so energetic, that the unnatural mode of indulging and satiating its cravings doubtless often occurs from the victim's own invention. Many have informed me, that they have fallen into it of their own will, having received no intimation of the practice from any other person; a greater number, unquestionably, are led into the vice by the example and instruction of their boyish companions, and as many, it is to be feared, from the iniquitous and premeditated counsels of grown up persons. One of the most dreadful cases ever occurring in my practice, a man who struggled, and fought, and prayed, against the ruin he had brought upon himself by long-continued indulgence in this habit, assured me, that an uncle had learned him the foul art, at an age anterior to that of puberty. And I have reason to believe, that in New England, within a few years, a teacher of a school, wonderfully popular in its day, an unmarried debauchee,[25] had the guilt of teaching some of the finest boys entrusted to his care by anxious parents, his odious and polluting sin. So infatuated were some of the poor victims of this hoary[26] sinner's depravity, that they were wont, as one of them told me, to quarrel amongst themselves, for the privilege of lodging within this unclean beast's den! Depraved or ignorant servants, hired men, and even female domestics and nurses, so say the French books, have been known to teach this vice to their tender and unsuspecting charge, and have thus inflicted on the hopes of parents, and the prospects of families, a blasting, scathing blow, of which oftentimes the recipients and the agents have been alike unconscious. . . .

Chapter V. Symptoms and Manifestations of Its Existence

In order to give a more graphic illustration of a case of *onanomania,*—for it will at least answer my convenience, so to designate it,—let us view the confirmed masturbator in the middle of his career. He will probably be found in full flesh and strength, often fat and bloated, with a good appetite and unimpaired digestion. You will, in his aspect, at first, notice little indications of disease. . . . The functions under the dominion of disease have been the nervous, and not the nutritive. There is exhaustion, but it is that nervous sensation of fatigue which prevails when the excitability of the system has been expended in labor, and not recruited by sleep; but not that feeling of debility, which arises from the sanguineous or nutritive organs being inadequately supplied, as from loss of blood, want of food, and the like. It is a sensation like that experienced by a person when a fever is taking hold of him; one day he may be in perfect health, and on the next, find himself, from mere nervous exhaustion, with no loss of flesh, too languid and feeble to maintain himself erect. There is muscular strength enough latent in the body, but it is kept prostrate by

---

[25] A person who is habituated to indulgence in sensual pleasures.
[26] Aged, derived from old age's association with white hair.

this unnatural draught upon the nervous influence. Rouse the masturbator into a passion, or let his own internal, diseased emotions and impulses call up his dormant energies, and you will find him far from being the enfeebled invalid you were formerly led to suppose.

I deem this a very important fact in its bearings, as being so diametrically opposed to the popular idea, as far as any obtains, on this point. The victim of the habit, and his parent, may alike be thrown off their guard, by supposing that they shall notice, in the diminished and decayed bodily energies, the traces of the habit. Wait not for these; they may exist, or they may be absent; its ravages are perhaps concentrating upon a far more noble and important portion of the being; the all-important, though mysterious functions of the brain and nervous system. . . .

Frequently, one of the earliest indications of the habit is an unwillingness to engage in the common, active, exciting plays of boys; instead of traversing over the whole face of the country, climbing rocks and trees, playing at ball, skating and the like, the boy selects some trashy novel, or sedentary amusement, because that energy and excitability of the system, which nature instinctively requires to be worked off in muscular exercise, has been expended, exhausted, wasted, in this unnaturally debilitating process. If engaged in play, the power of running will be found less than it is on the average, and the breathing is soon affected.

This same nervous exhaustion displays itself in a constant disposition to assume a recumbent position; to loll about on chairs, or the sofa; to lay on the bed in the day time, not for the purpose of sleeping, but to gratify this feeling of weakness; to read in bed at night, and to continue in bed in the morning, after being awakened.

The mind becomes fascinated with the morbid gratification of exciting and libidinous readings and imaginings; the power of fixing the attention steadily and deeply is lost; and of grappling with any thing that is abstruse in studies. The imagination runs riot; day dreams, fanciful castle-building in the air, involving especially the sensual, usurp the place of the practical, and common sense views of things. Yet in many instances, it is as extraordinary, as it is generally unsuspected, how far the *intellectual* faculties, as evinced in ordinary conversations, are unimpaired, even in the last stages of apparent dementia. . . .

It is to the moral and affective characteristics of the individual, that I believe generally the ravages of this vice are directed. In its early stages, the manner will be found unnatural. The boy is unwilling to look the person addressing him in the eye. Upon this alone too much stress ought not to be placed, as bashfulness is so common a trait even amongst the purest boys; but, in conjunction with others, it is well worth being noticed by the tender and anxious parents.

I have also considered, as one of the most usual proofs of a young man's having fallen into this debasing practice, an unwillingness and disinclination to enjoy the society of young persons of the other sex. The youth of ten or a dozen years usually has, it is true, a timid shyness and embarrassment, in the company of young females. But, as he advances in age, nothing can be more in accordance with the laws of nature, with the pure, unsullied dictates of instinct and reason, than the commencement of a disposition to court the society of woman.

Chapter VI. Influences on the Moral and Physical Character, Further Illustrated

... Multitudes of young men, who have left our colleges and other seminaries of learning, with the full persuasion of themselves and their friends and instructers, that they were the victims of hard study, have in fact been only the victims of solitary pollution. There is nothing in study, as pursued in this country, calculated to overthrow the constitution, and destroy the health. ...

I have known repeated instances, where the disease has taken his turn. The young man, abandoning his employment, whether of labor or study, returns to his father's house,—loses all his energy and enterprise of mind and body,—hangs about in listless idleness, under the pretence, on his own and his friends' part, of his suffering from poor health. He is not exactly sick of any specific or named disease; for he has a good appetite, sleeps more hours than is natural, and has no occasion for the services of the medical attendant to repair any palpable deviations from health; but he is dronish, irritable, suspicious and unhappy. He may take to his bed, and lay recumbent most of his time; avoids seeing any person, as far as possible. During these manifestations, he may not be deemed, by the world, exactly insane, for there is no apparent intellectual aberration,—no delusions,—no false fancies, at least, that are obvious; but he is perhaps deemed *love-cracked* or *hypoish*.[27] Such individuals may, after a while, adopt some

---

[27] *Hypoish* is not a known word, but from its use here is probably a shortened version of hypochondriacal, meaning, in the nineteenth century, someone afflicted with a morbid state of mind, characterized by low spirits, for which there was no medically perceivable cause.

delusive idea, and become decidedly deranged on some one point, that is monomaniac.[28] This mania will probably bear some relation to injuries intended, or in suspicions of their best friends, or of persons with whom they have no acquaintance. They threaten revenge, and even attempt violence, and thus compel their friends, or the public authorities, to confine them, beyond the power of doing mischief. Such has been the history of many of those, who are now in our asylums for the insane, where they constitute not only the most hopelessly incurable class (probably not five cases in a hundred from masturbation ever recovering), but a class the most dangerous, troublesome and disgusting.

[28]A person suffering from a form of mental illness characterized by focus on a single fixed idea or act.

11

MARY S. GOVE [NICHOLS]

From *Solitary Vice*

1839

Mary S. Gove (1810–1884) addressed her concerns about masturbation to women in particular. She started out as a disciple of Sylvester Graham, accepting both his physiological system and his deep anxiety about masturbation, and, under his influence, she wrote Solitary Vice. *She became a lecturer on the body to female audiences, using a mannequin for illustration. By the end of the first phase of her work, Gove emerged as a leading proponent of the water cure, a therapy particularly important to female followers.*

... When I commenced my invsetigations [sic] on this subject, I was not at all prepared for the state of things that met my view. I was not prepared to believe that the vice was at all common among females.

Mary Sargeant Gove [Nichols], *Solitary Vice: An Address to Parents and Those Who Have the Care of Children* (Portland, Maine: Journal Office, 1839).

But I have been obliged to believe what numbers have told me of themselves. Some of the most lovely and conscientious females I have ever met, have confessed to me that they had been victims of this habit. They were ignorant of its turpitude, of its moral and physical effects. Information was alone wanting to save these individuals from a state of health which made life itself a burden. Again I ask, shall we withhold correct information from our children, and leave them to the teaching of the enemy of all good and their own depraved passions?

A christian female has given me the following confession, which she permits me to use as I deem best for the good of her sex:

DEAR MRS. G.—I believe you are engaged in an important and holy work, and my heart's desire and prayer to God is that you may long be spared to prosecute it. It has been neglected till the world is filled with misery and crime. An imperative sense of duty constrains me to communicate some facts that may tend to encourage you, to convince the skeptical, and to arouse those who have the supervision of youth to greater faithfulness and assiduity. When very young I became addicted to self pollution, and continued it for several years, and but for a merciful Providence that made me a subject of converting grace, and an early marriage, I might now be suffering all its concomitant evils.* Allow me to offer a few thoughts respecting the vice. I believe it is *very prevalent*, though for many years I supposed it *confined to myself.* Recent facts have fearfully demonstrated the reverse.**[29] I was *most religiously* educated. My parents endeavored to make me *feel* the holiness of the law and its obligations. But the seventh commandment was overlooked.[30] Thus was I left, the untaught child of nature, exposed to the unchecked dictates of a depraved heart and corrupt associates. It was unsuspected by my parents. I suppose if I were now to state these facts to them they would hardly credit them. I always supposed I contracted this practice instinctively, till recently, a friend who is several years older than myself, informed me that at the age of *four* years she taught me.†

---

*She had suffered much, but owing to her early abandonment of the practice she had obtained tolerable health.

†This friend has continued the practice, in single and married life, until she had wrecked her constitution and made life a burden; and a burden which she must soon lay down.

[29] In the original text, the stars are likely for emphasis.

[30] The *seventh commandment*—Thou shalt not commit adultery—was broadly interpreted in this era to forbid all sexual expression outside of marriage, including premarital intercourse and, here, masturbation.

This lady goes on to make some farther statements respecting the prevalence of the practice, which go to confirm the truth of the preceding pages. Almost all those who have confessed to me, that they had been guilty of this practice, who had not been taught the vice, say they thought they were *the only* individuals in the world who practiced it. I think a majority of those who have communicated with me on this subject had not been taught the vice, and knew not that any other person practised it. Doubtless their parents considered them both ignorant and innocent. Perhaps they thought the safety of these very children consisted in keeping them ignorant. I was once conversing with a mother on these subjects and striving to awaken an interest in her mind, when she remarked with much earnestness, "I believe my child is pure." I had that very child's confession at that time, and knew that she had practised the sin for years, and nearly lost her life by it; and yet her mother believed her pure, and no doubt had felt that it would have corrupted her daughter to communicate this information to her.

Parents are prone to put this evil afar off: to say, my child is pure. But let every mother warn her children, and instruct them faithfully; let her rest assured that no harm can result from it, and in almost every instance it will do good, either by saving the children from falling, or through their means saving others. I knew a young woman who had got some information on this subject, by reading the best book on the subject ever published, viz. Graham's Lecture to young men, and she resolved to inform her only brother. . . .

The hope of society is in the youth, and our hope for our youth is, under God, in a correct course of training, as respects diet and regimen, instruction and warning. Parents should do all in their power, by education, to form right habits, and to prevent the formation of wrong habits. Grace alone can renovate the heart. The present unhealthy and stimulating method of living, prematurely developes the passions, and continually urges to their gratification. Almost all the present habits of civil life are calculated to produce such results. The neglect of bathing, of exercise, the use of soft feather beds, and often the too great abundance of clothing—the use of condiments, pepper, spice, and indeed all heating and stimulating substances, whether solid or fluid; the habitual want of confidence between parents and children; the false delicacy almost every where cultivated—all have their influence in bringing about this lamentable state of things. Generally speaking, schools are nurseries of vice.

A short time since, two sisters, ladies of the first respectability, informed me that when very young they were put to a Female Boarding School, where this vice prevailed, and the practice was explained to them. They were blessed with parents who were willing to converse with and warn their children, and they escaped contamination. The best way to guard our children from this vice, is to make their diet plain from the cradle; to exclude all rich and high-seasoned food, meats, pastry, confectionary, &c. from their diet; bathe them thoroughly every day in cold water, or if they be very delicate, in slightly warm water; let them sleep on a mattress, or straw, but in no case on feathers. Let them exercise daily in the open air; clothe them properly, but not with flannel next to skin, unless in cases of disease, when recommended by a Physician. Instruct and warn them; cultivate a spirit of kindness and confidence toward them; listen to their little complaints of what they meet from their mates. I have heard the most disgusting conversation, when a child, from school children, and yet I dared not tell my mother. Many parents will not hear a word of complaint from their children. "Don't tell me tales," say they. The poor child must bear all in silence. Judicious confidence will never foster a spirit of tale-telling.

We have been unjust to children long enough. It is time we act efficiently for their benefit, if we would save our children.

12

CHARLES KNOWLTON

Gonorrhoea Dormientium

August 10, 1842

Charles Knowlton was an unusual voice of reason during the masturbation panic. He retained his free-thinking ways throughout his life. Publishing this article in the Boston Medical and Surgical Journal *was an indication that he had won respect in the Massachusetts medical community. Knowlton wrote in an era in which many believed that what*

Charles Knowlton, "Gonorrhoea Dormientium," *Boston Medical and Surgical Journal* 27, no. 1 (August 10, 1842): 11–15.

were later called "wet dreams" were serious pathological symptoms caused by masturbation.

To the Editor of the Boston Medical and Surgical Journal

Sir,—For good and sufficient reason my thoughts have been directed to the subject of nocturnal seminal emissions for more than twenty years. . . .

Gonorrhoea Dormientium is a disease (or symptom?) which may exist to a great extent without being attended with any distinct pains; yet few diseases render their subject more extremely wretched. I believe its pathology and treatment are not well understood by the profession. It is far from being a rare disease, and it rightly belongs to the province of medicine. . . .

Nocturnal emissions so generally occur during a libidinous dream, that it is reasonable to suppose they always do so, although the dream may not always be re-called when awake. They occur mostly in young men, and are attended with erection and a pleasurable sensation, except in a few cases of unusual severity. The emission takes place ten times more speedily on the occurrence of the dream, than it would were the person awake and actually engaged in the scenes and acts of which he dreams. This fact is often a source of sad and depressing reflection to *inexperienced* young men. They erroneously think that the real act would cause an emission much more speedily than a mere dream, and, of course, that they are disqualified for giving or receiving much pleasure with a female. Another sad reflection, at least with the male subjects of this disease, is that they have brought it upon themselves by the vicious practice of masturbation. . . . A third erroneous and very depressing reflection with some of these patients is, not only that they are incapacitated for giving and receiving pleasure, to any considerable extent, but that it would be destructive to their very lives to do so, even if they could; or, in few words, that it would kill them to marry. Great good may be done these patients by setting them right on all these points. It is of no use to look gravely, and tell them that their case is a very bad one. I make light of it, and laugh a load of melancholy out of them. I take down Blumenbach's Physiology, London Edition, 1815, and turn to page 208, where we read as follows—"I regard these nocturnal pollutions as among the natural secretions, intended to liberate the system from the otherwise urgent superfluous semen, more or less frequently, according to the variety of temperament and constitution." I tell the young unmarried men—unless they are dying off with consumption or some other disease—to marry as soon as convenient; and I assure you, Mr. Editor, that I have known this advice to be followed in several instances, and always with success. . . .

Allow me now to offer a few speculations on the etiology and pathology of these nocturnal emissions. I regard the term "seminal weakness," by which they are sometimes designated, as erroneous in theory and mischievous in practice. It is *irritability* rather than debility of the genital organs, that co-operates with the brain or the "imagination," in the production of these discharges. These organs are in such a ticklish, sensitive state, that the presence of semen in the seminal vessels . . . makes an undue impression upon them, and this impression being conveyed to the brain, sets the individual to "thinking about these things." He dreams of being in the company of a female, and what is a little curious and inexplicable, he ever finds her a "non-resistant." The imagination now re-acts powerfully and concentratedly—for outward impressions and internal reflections do not interfere as when all the cerebral organs are active or awake—upon the irritable genital organs, and thus the emission is speedily produced. . . .

It appears then, according to the foregoing speculations, that irritability of the genital organs plays a very important part in the production of involuntary seminal emissions. But what causes this morbid irritability? It is not debility; for these emissions generally occur for the first time, and often continue to occur occasionally, in cases where there is no indication of debility in any part of the system. They are not cured by stimulants, tonics and astringents, but sometimes made worse by them, while they are generally benefited by medicines of a very different class; and we are daily seeing patients extremely debilitated throughout the whole system, without being at all subject to these emissions. Nor do I admit that masturbation is the sole cause of this irritability (but the irritability may lead to masturbation), and for the following reasons. First, masturbation is practised by thousands who are not subject to these emissions, and practised to a greater extent, too, than it ever has been by many who are subject to them. Second, in some cases certainly, and probably in most, as soon as these involuntary emissions occur, the young man is alarmed, and relinquishes at once and entirely the practice of onanism; but no cures—I presume to say not a single cure—were ever obtained in this way. . . .

I tell my patients that as the habit of secretion is established in the testicles, they must not expect to be wholly exempt from involuntary emissions so long as they do not practise voluntary ones. I do not, however, advise them to go back to the practice of masturbation, but tell them to let their involuntary emissions come along, if they will, and not think or care anything about them. I tell them that if they cannot otherwise divert and direct their minds, and cease to think on certain subjects, which thinking is a perpetual stimulus to the genital organs, they must marry. This will soothe their nerves, becalm the whole body and mind, take off the local irritation of seminal repletion, supersede involuntary emissions, about which they have been so much troubled, and finally restore them to perfect health. If they seem to doubt, I tell them to doubt not, for I speak from *personal* as well as from practical experience. . . .

NEW VOICES AT MID-CENTURY

13

WILLIAM ANDRUS ALCOTT

From *The Physiology of Marriage*
1856

By the 1850s, there were many voices deliberating sex in print. Health reformer William Andrus Alcott (1798–1859) was a teacher, physician, and writer who promoted education and healthy living in numerous books. He positioned himself within the Christian wing of reform physiology to continue the work of Sylvester Graham. As might be expected, he championed sexual restraint in marriage and abstinence outside it. He also wrote against abortion and the application of any contraceptive technique other than what a later generation called the "rhythm method." He was the cousin of Amos Bronson Alcott, the utopian founder of Fruitlands, and his daughter Louisa May Alcott, author of Little Women.

William A. Alcott, *The Physiology of Marriage* (Boston: John P. Jewett & Co., 1856).

Preface

... To the publication of such a work [as this book on the physiology of marriage] I know of but one general objection which the wise will be likely to urge. It is that one or two of its chapters are not so well adapted to the wants of mere boys, as to those of youth and young men; while the former will be most eager to read them. The proper reply to such an objection—specious as it seems to be—is that the field is pre-occupied. If it were desirable to keep boys, for a few years, in ignorance on the subjects alluded to, it could not be done. Satan already has his emissaries abroad, in various shapes; and they are as active as if they were employed in a more worthy cause. What is left to the friends of God and humanity, as it appears to me, is to counteract his plans, by extending the domain of conscience over that part of the Divine Temple which has too often been supposed not to be under law, but to be the creature of blind instinct, in which we are only on a par with the beasts that perish. . . .

Individual Transgression and Its Penalties

... Young men of fifteen or sixteen years, on finding themselves in possession of new powers of enjoyment, easily flatter themselves that, however it may be with *others,* they are in no danger of impairing those powers. What ardently we wish, we soon believe. And what, in the ardor of youth, we honestly believe, we are eloquent to defend.

And their reasoning is specious. God has given us the appetite, say they, and the means of its gratification; but why so, if it is not to be indulged? Perhaps they have a smattering of such knowledge as some of the books and schools have been wont to teach, and have called it physiology. As the existence of the tears, saliva, pancreatic juice, etc., with the curious machinery which forms them, imply an object to be accomplished, say they, why should not the existence of a fluid in the testicles, with the accompanying machinery for its formation or secretion, imply an object, too? In other words, as the existence of the saliva, gastric juice, etc., prove that we ought to eat, why do not the existence of the genitals and their accompanying secretion prove that these organs ought to be occasionally exercised?

But there is a difference between the two. All the fluids connected with the apparatus for the digestion of our food, have for their object the well being of the individual and the continuance of his existence.

The seminal fluid and its machinery on the contrary have nothing to do, directly, with sustaining the life and health of the individual. There are even not wanting in the records of men and things, facts which go far towards proving that the life and health of an individual considered without reference to his duties or relations to others, would be quite as well sustained without any indulgence of the sexual propensity, as *with* that indulgence, even though it were in the greatest moderation. . . .

The reader will not, of course, understand me as reasoning against marriage, in the abstract; especially as I have already insisted on it as a primary duty. . . .

It is equally unquestionable, moreover, that God has, in the nature and constitution of things, set a limit to the indulgence of the sexual appetite somewhere short of our ability to gratify it. He has done so with the other appetites; why should he not with this? . . .

The Physical Laws of Marriage

. . . Did fathers hold familiar conversation with their sons, and mothers with their daughters, on this important subject, and did the young make their parents their oracles instead of trusting to sources of information, which, at best, are very questionable, we should not find so many of both sexes rushing within the precincts of this sacred enclosure as ignorant of the first principles of matrimonial law as if no such law had ever existed. . . .

The first question asked by inquiring young men, who are fairly within the matrimonial enclosure, usually is, "What is right, with regard to sexual intercourse?" "Here we are," say they, "with our appetites and passions urging us on; and yet we are fully assured there is a limit which we ought not to pass. Tell us, if you can, where that limit is."

But, in order to reply, in the best possible manner, to such a question as this, much time is required. . . .

. . . Twenty years ago I asked a most excellent man, of great age, observation, and experience—one, moreover, whose praise was in "all the churches," what he should regard as matrimonial excess. He hesitated, at first. Much, he said, would depend on circumstances. What would be excess in one person of a certain temperament and of a particular age, would be but moderation in another. . . . However, he concluded at length, that as a general rule, any thing beyond twice a week, for him and his companion, would be excess.

On relating this conversation, sometime afterward, (of course without giving names) to an experienced physician, he remarked, that as many indulgences as two in a week would destroy him and many others—persons even of average constitutions. . . .

Some of my readers may perhaps be already aware that the far-famed, and very far-hated, Sylvester Graham taught a doctrine [of one sexual indulgence a month]. . . .

This doctrine, it is true, so utterly at war with the general habits and feelings of mankind, was almost enough, at the time it was announced, to provoke the cry of, Crucify him. Indeed, I have often thought that while the public odium was ostensibly directed against his anti-fine flour and anti-flesh eating doctrines, it was his anti-sexual indulgence doctrines, in reality, which excited the public hatred and rendered his name a by-word and a reproach. . . .

On this point, however, I speak, as it becomes me, with some diffidence. For, I am by no means sure that our most ultra physiologists are not very near the truth, after all. I am by no means certain that Scripture revelation—to say nothing of physiology—in its most rigid interpretation, does not restrict us to the simple purpose of perpetuating the race. I am, however, quite sure that one indulgence to each lunar month, is all that the best health of the parties can possibly require. . . .

But young men, as we have seen, are usually without information; and hence seem to suppose that within the pale of matrimonial life there is no limit to indulgence except that which grows out of a due respect for woman—rather, I should perhaps say, to a good and faithful beast of burden—and some degree of regard to their own immediate suffering. Hence it is that the first months of matrimonial life are, so often, little better than a season of prostitution, except that it has not yet been stigmatized with the name. Hence, too, one reason why we have so many still born, prematurely born, and sickly children; as well as why we lose one half of all who are born under ten years of age. . . .

I have alluded to the opinion, quite common with the young of our sex, that marriage is, or may be, a state of unrestrained intercourse. So far is it from being the design of the great author of this institution, to render it a scene of unlicensed indulgence, or, in other words, of habitual, practical prostitution, that I have no doubt the intention was the reverse of all this. Instead of encouraging indulgence without limit, one of its very designs appears to me to teach us self-restraint and self-denial. Nor could the Divine Being give us, as far as I can see, a more favorable school for this purpose.

Man, to repeat what has been repeatedly affirmed, already, is coarse and sensual—he needs to be polished and purified. Both of these offices, marriage, when rightly understood and properly regarded, never fails to accomplish. It does not require celibacy or the nunnery on the one hand, nor does it permit indulgence on the other. It simply requires us to be men and women; but it demands that we should be rational men and women, and not mere brutes. Above all, it does not permit us to be brutes of the lowest and most degraded cast. . . .

Crimes without Name

Every man knows, or ought to know, that the great object of the sexual function is the reproduction of the species; and though not all the seed which is cast into the human soil is expected to germinate and grow, yet when it does spring up and bring forth, he is bound to take care of it; and the younger and more delicate the germ, or the shoot, the greater is his obligation to rear it and nurture it, even till it reaches maturity.

This, I have by figure, called a tax. Is such taxation tyrannous? . . . Is the promise of the future, in the case of human reproduction, of less value [than the produce of our farms]?

Some appear to regard it so; indeed, many do.—They wish for full liberty to scatter their seed; it is a pleasure to them, a luxury to which they seem to think themselves entitled; but they do not wish to have a crop. It would be burdensome to them. A mow of wheat or rye, or a bin of corn they would highly prize; but a family of children they do not want. . . .

Hence it is that ways, almost innumerable, are devised for evading nature's laws altogether. . . . They are all criminal, even though they should be, as they seem to be, crimes without names.

Some twenty or twenty-five years ago, a physician of New England [Dr. Charles Knowlton], of much greater practical skill than strict integrity, especially towards God, became the author of a small pocket volume, with a very inviting title [*Fruits of Philosophy*], whose avowed object was to teach people, both in married life and elsewhere, the art of gratifying the sexual appetite without the necessity of progeny. His book had a wide circulation. I have found it in nearly every part of our wide-spread country.

It was the more successful, no doubt, from the fact that the author declared his chemical mixture or lotion to be not only certain in its preventive effects, if applied immediately, but entirely uninjurious to the delicate tissues against which it was injected. It is in vogue, even now, in many parts of our country, and is highly prized. They, who have tried it, usually regard it as entirely certain in its effects; though I have reason to doubt the soundness of this conclusion. . . .

But of all the measures for accomplishing these results which I have called *crimes without name,* none are more common, I think, than the use of poison of one kind or another, and that of instruments; and certainly none are more reprehensible. True it is, that if done with the same intention, crime is crime, at any period of foetal development; and not less so at conception. Still there is something peculiarly shocking in those cases of destruction which approximate to maturity of the embryo, especially when the results are accomplished by poison, or by surgical instruments. . . .

True it is that many who find themselves pregnant resort to tradition and household practice for what they call relief. Some field, or swamp, or grove contains the needful poison; and forthwith it is swallowed. Sometimes life is destroyed as the result;—I mean, now, the life of the principal offender—but it happens, much more frequently, that she escapes with less injury than her offspring. . . .

It seems to be a well known physiological law that conception cannot take place at every period of female life between the catamenial[31] discharges; but only during the first fortnight, or as some say, the first eight days which immediately follow the cessation of the menses. If, therefore, we deny ourselves, during a full fortnight as above mentioned, no subsequent intercourse, up to the commencement of the next catamenial discharge, can possibly be productive.

You will observe that I have been stating in the last paragraph, a generally received opinion; and not a mere surmise of my own. Whether the course which is thus indicated is right or not, is quite another question. . . .

---

[31] *Catamenial* is a term that means menstrual.

14

LORENZO N. FOWLER

From *The Principles of Phrenology and Physiology Applied to Man's Social Relations*
1842

Phrenology became an important voice in the public discussion of sex in the 1850s. Based on the theories of Viennese physician Franz Joseph Gall and brought to America by Johann Spurzheim in 1832, phrenology was a science of the mind that held that the brain was made up of separate parts, each governing a specific aspect of character. Lorenzo Niles Fowler (1811–1896) and his brother Orson were its leading proponents in the United States. By asserting that the cerebellum at the base of the brain contained an organ of "amativeness," the source of the reproductive instinct, phrenology declared sexual passion to be natural and legitimate. Phrenological understandings made it possible for adherents to discuss in print the physical as well as the emotional aspects of lovemaking.

Phrenology and Physiology as Applied to Marriage

Man was created with the express design of becoming perfectly happy, both *physically* and *mentally*. But in order to enjoy this boon of Heaven, he must understand and obey the laws of his being, and give to every power of his mind and body just that kind of exercise and direction which their nature requires. . . .

Not only the happiness, but the very existence of man depends on a union of the sexes. This is a law of our nature—a part of our being, and involves some of the most important objects for which we were placed in this world. The institution of marriage is, moreover, sanctioned by Heaven, and it is, therefore, right and proper that we should make ourselves thoroughly acquainted with the nature of this institution, as well as the relations growing out of it. . . .

L. N. Fowler, *The Principles of Phrenology and Physiology Applied to Man's Social Relations; Together with an Analysis of the Domestic Feelings* (New York: L. N. and O. S. Fowler, 1842).

Phrenology and physiology are the only sciences which make us acquainted with the laws of our organization, and afford that kind of knowledge by which we may comply with them to the best advantage.

Physiology makes us acquainted with those conditions of the body upon which long life and health depend, as well as with what physical qualities our own are best adapted.

Phrenology makes us acquainted with the faculties of the mind and their manifestations. . . .

The domestic feelings and propensities are located in that portion of the head which is occupied by the lower and posterior convolutions of the brain—mostly covered by the occipital bone. Their influence upon character is greater than any other given number of faculties, and they occupy a larger portion of the brain. And these faculties, properly or improperly directed, have more to do with the happiness or misery of mankind than any other class; hence the importance of securing their proper influence and direction. They being very strong and active, are *extremely* liable to be perverted, particularly by young persons, in whom they are excitable, and who have had but little experience in the world. The most effectual way to direct these feelings in the proper channel, and prevent their becoming perverted, is to secure the equal exercise of the moral and intellectual faculties, allowing the social feelings to be freely exercised in virtuous society, innocent amusements, and reading suitable books—thus creating a balance of power in favor of intelligence, morality and virtue.

The first faculty called into exercise in the social group, is AMATIVENESS, situated in the cerebellum, giving width between and behind the ears. . . .

Its function and manifestation is adapted to and in harmony with the condition of man and animals, as agents of reproduction. It gives us all those feelings and impulses which we experience between the sexes, as such. "It exerts a quiet, but effectual influence in the general intercourse between the sexes, giving rise in each to a sort of kindly interest in all that concerns the other. It softens all the proud, irascible and antisocial principles of our nature, in every thing which regards that sex which is the object of it; and it increases the activity and force of all the kindly and benevolent affections. This explains many facts which appear in the mutual regards of the sexes towards each other. Men are, generally speaking, more generous and kind, more benevolent and charitable, toward women, than they are to men, or than women are to one another." The characters of both sexes are improved by the society of the other, by way of making man modest, polite and refined, and woman more energetic, ambitious and talented. In healthy and well-formed persons, the larger the organ, the more desirable is the company of the other sex. It is much influenced by the imagination in increasing the charms and personal attractions where there are but few, thus giving false impressions of each other, and directing the intellect into a wrong channel. But if the organ is small, the person is less susceptible to emotions of love; is cold-hearted and distant—disposed to avoid the company of the opposite sex, and manifests a want of refinement, tenderness, warmth and delicacy of feeling, which should exist between the sexes. The affections of such a person may be characterized by purity of feeling and platonic attachment, rather than by those impassioned emotions which spring from large Amativeness.

This faculty is very much affected by the temperament, and under peculiar circumstances may be so much excited as, for the time being, to appear large, when it is in fact only moderate.

This faculty should be equal in its influences between the parties united, in order to secure the greatest amount of happiness in domestic life and the harmonious exercise of all the other faculties—for a majority of the difficulties which occur between man and wife arise from the irregular and unequal influences of this faculty.

When the function of this faculty is perverted, it leads to looseness, licentiousness, vulgarity, low life and profligacy. Hence, we see individuals of high standing and rank in society, and distinguished for intellectual and sometimes for moral greatness, become *very* degraded in the eyes of the virtuous, when guided by the perverted influences of this faculty. The whole history of man, in sacred and profane history, and in all gradations of society, bears strong and degrading marks of its perversion; and in no possible way does human nature appear so low and disgusting, so brutal and devoid of reason, as when this faculty has the controlling influence—a faculty which, guided by reason and modified by the moral sentiments, is calculated to secure the highest degree of domestic enjoyment, and make social life most pleasant and desirable. But, strange as it may appear, human nature has become so depraved, the intellect and ambition of many influential men are so misdirected that they consider their greatness and popularity to increase in proportion to the perversion of this faculty, thus leading thousands astray. It is the part and natural influence of Phrenology, to exert a great influence in correcting these false impressions, and bringing about a very important reform in this matter.

This faculty is stronger in the male than in the female, and in them more often perverted. The more common ways which lead to the excitement and perversion of this faculty are:

First. The indulgence of the appetite in the too free use of stimulating food and drink in connnection with the exercise of the social feelings—such as parties of pleasure, clubs, carouses, balls, &c. The fashion of honoring men and measures, of celebrating party triumphs or birthdays by superb dinners and late suppers of the most rich food, of passing around the glass so freely and allowing the merits of the cause which they honor to be a sufficient excuse for becoming intoxicated, is decidedly bad, or has an immoral tendency. For a proof of this, we have only to notice the persons who encourage them, and see the consequences of such a course of education. The evil is twofold: one is, that it makes drunkards; the other is, it encourages licentiousness.

Secondly. Encouraging certain modes of dress calculated expressly to attract the attention of the opposite sex, and exciting the curiosity by the peculiar manner in which dress envelops the female form—arousing the passion in those who have it strong, and the disgust of those more elevated in feeling. All may be considered as the legitimate effects of many of the now existing fashions.

Thirdly. Reading works of romance written by persons of morbid feelings, sickly sentiments and extravagant hopes—all containing highly wrought scenes of amatory happiness and earthly felicity—thus exciting the feelings and weakening the judgment, creating a distaste for commonplace transactions, and giving false and imperfect ideas of human nature.

Fourthly. Attending theatres and other similar places of amusement, whose principal attractions now are, unnatural and far-fetched representations of scenes overloaded with "love," in sentiment and in action, the most absurd, because unreal. In truth, it may well be called *acting.* Besides, at these places there are resorts where licentiousness stalks openly and defyingly, where the most abandoned congregate, a moral Upas tree, which disseminates all impurity and blights with deadly and destructive effect the moral feelings.

And again, there are many other more private ways of its perversion which different individuals resort to under various circumstances. Its perverted influences are very contagious and easily felt, as most persons in society are aware. . . . An individual in whom this faculty is perverted, is constantly exerting a contaminating influence over all his associates, and he is successful in leading others astray, in proportion as he can control their minds. Most of the chit-chat talk of young ladies and gentlemen, when they are striving to entertain each other most successfully, has a demoralizing influence, and should be discountenanced.

Much exertion is made at the present day, to reform mankind in regard to this faculty, but a complete and radical reformation cannot take place until we understand thoroughly the design, function and adaptation of this faculty; and the causes of its perversion being known are guarded against until this faculty of the mind receives its proper attention as well as the moral and intellectual faculties. Parents and teachers must lay aside their false delicacy, and teach their children in relation to the full and important bearings of the seventh commandment, how to obey it, thus cultivating this as well as the other faculties of the mind, and discountenancing its too early and improper manifestations, taking particular care to fill their minds with useful and virtuous thoughts. This faculty becomes wrongly directed in children much earlier than many are aware. Many facts have come under my observation of its perverted influences, in children from four years old and upwards. More attention should be paid to the *early* manifestations of this faculty, in order to secure its proper direction, for it is one of the strongest feelings of our nature, and when once perverted or improperly biassed, the morals of such an individual are on a sandy foundation, and receive a fundamental and permanent injury.

15

LORENZO N. FOWLER

From *Marriage: Its History and Ceremonies*

1846

Lorenzo Fowler published widely on phrenological understandings and, along with his brother, became a leading counselor on sexual matters in the mid-nineteenth century. With the outset of the Civil War, he moved with his physician wife, Lydia, to set up a branch of the Fowler firm in London.

Lorenzo N. Fowler, *Marriage: Its History and Ceremonies; with a Phrenological and Physiological Exposition of the Functions and Qualifications for Happy Marriages* (New York: Fowler and Wells, 1846).

Love: What Is It? — How Secured, How Retained, and Its Natural Language

The term LOVE, is applied so universally, abstractly, and generally, that it means almost any thing that we may wish. It has every variety of signification, every shade of meaning which any one has a mind to attach to it. The term love, as it is generally used, is applied to all pleasurable emotions, whether physical or mental. . . .

The term "perfect love," as applied to a true union of two in marriage, is something more than the above. It comprises more than all united loves. . . . Without it, mankind are miserable; with it, perfectly happy. . . . Those who are fully imbued with it, are honest, virtuous, industrious, moral, refined, and elevated in feeling and conduct, and are happy and contented. Those who do not possess it, are discontented, unhappy, irregular in their habits and feelings, and more or less inclined to wander and yield to immoral practices.

Married persons who love each other always live together agreeably. Those who do not, are at variance; frequently have disputations, abuse each other beyond endurance, and separate as enemies.

Love embraces many qualities and conditions. It is on a graduating scale. It commences with the physical; and, when perfected, ends with the spiritual. With many, love goes no higher than the physical qualities; but, with a few, the physical has less charms than the mental. Spiritual love is enjoyed where one MIND is united to another in a union of sentiment and affection which no external defects can dissolve. Physical love arises from the appreciation of physical qualities, and the enjoyment of a physical union. Perfect love is a union of these two (physical and mental), with spiritual love in the ascendency, overruling and bringing into harmonious subjection all the propensities of our nature to the moral and intellectual faculties; or, in other words, it is the result of the union of two congenial spirits, in which all the faculties of the mind are gratified according to their legitimate natural functions and strength.

Much is said, at the present day, about spiritual love; also, of a first and only love; and their superiority over all others. Some affirm to me, that their love is purely spiritual; that they have no sympathy with the physical; but, in my opinion, such a mind is not well balanced; for, as long as we have a physical organization, we need a mind adapted to it; and, as many of the social duties of life require physical love, it is only in harmony with our natures and duties to possess it, and allow it to have its due influences in the mind; yet held in subordination to the higher elements . . . .

16

ORSON S. FOWLER

From *Love and Parentage*

1851

In 1832, Orson Squire Fowler (1809–1887) shifted from the ministry, for which he trained at Amherst College, to phrenology. In 1842, he moved to New York and with many family members established a successful phrenological enterprise that published books and journals; offered counseling for careers, marriage, and child raising; and sustained a museum open to the public.

All-Important Considerations to the Married: Reciprocity

LOVE always requires a RETURN. RECIPROCITY is a constituent ingredient in its very nature. Without it neither can ever be happy in either love or wedlock. Its absence is misery to the ardor of the one, and repugnance to the coldness of the other. A cardinal law of both love and connubial[32] bliss requires, that the more tender the affection of either, the more cordially should it be reciprocrated by the other. . . . Because parentage absolutely requires the joint participancy of two, a male and female, and allows only two to partake in the authorship of every single product of humanity, both of whom must necessarily thus partake together; therefore love, which is only an incipient and preparatory stage of parentage, must be reciprocal between two opposite sexes. Both must LOVE EACH OTHER, in order that both may participate with each other in this parental copartnership. As both must participate *together* in this repast of love, in order to render it productive, so both must cordially love each other as a preparation for this repast. . . . And in what consists the marriage vow, but in the implied and fully recognised act of convenanting with each other to participate together in this ultimate repast of love? Candidates for matrimony! what but this do you seek and proffer in forming this alliance?

[32]A synonym for married.

O. S. Fowler, *Love and Parentage, Applied to the Improvement of Offspring* (New York: Fowler and Wells, 1851).

Affected prudishness may pretend to frown upon this home truth; but, viewed in whatever light you please, the long and short, warp and woof, and sole imbodiment, of both love and matrimony—the one legitimate element, end, motive, and object desired and prompted—of either separately and of both collectively—consists in the anticipation and pledging of each to participate this function of love with the other. This is the origin of the marriage RITES. . . .

. . . The *happiness* conferred by each on the other being the sole occasion of love, and reciprocity here being the heart's-core of all the happiness of both love and wedlock—their basis, and frame-work, and superstructure, and *all in all—therefore* those who are qualified to confer on each other this *summum bonum*[33] of matrimonial felicity, are bound together by the strongest bond of union connected with our nature; whilst those who cannot both confer and receive mutual pleasure in this respect cannot possibly be happy in married life, and consequently cannot possibly love each other; and therefore should never enter together the sacred enclosure of wedlock. . . .

But, nothing will sting him so severely with disappointment, despair, and hatred, as unsatisfied desire. The reason is this. As already seen, Amativeness, the cerebral organ of this passion, bears the most intimate relation to the whole body, and the entire mentality, as the means of the propagation of both. Hence, its gratification abates that burning fever consequent on its unsatisfied cravings, and calms down that irritability of the animal propensities, which always necessarily accompanies its reversed and painful action. . . .

. . . But its *denial,* fires up to their highest pitch of abnormal and therefore depraved manifestation, the whole of the animal region, the body included; and thus produces sin and misery in their most aggravated forms. . . .

First, to the reluctant wife! For you to *yield,* is to conquer. By showing a desire to do all you can to oblige a beseeching husband, you throw yourself on his *generosity,* and thereby quell that desire which coldness or refusal would only aggravate. Your cheerful submission to what he knows to be disagreeable at once excites his pity and gratitude, and thus awakens his higher faculties in your behalf, and subdues desire; because, how *can* he who dotes on you take pleasure in what occasions you pain? He takes your *will* for the deed, and loves you therefore too well to insist on so delicate a matter unless agreeable to you also, or to feast himself at your expense. Compliance is a

---

[33]Latin for "the supreme good."

sovereign remedy for his importunity, because it *kills his desires.* Remember, you must always yield *cheerfully,* and with a view to *please him,* or else the whole effect will be lost. Never prove remiss, but do all you can to conform. Thereby you will lay your husband under the highest possible obligations of love and gratitude; whereas the unkind *refusal* begets increased importunity, and makes him *insist on his rights,* and threaten you with vengeance if you dare refuse. Abundant excuse, such as the most unreasonable demand on his part, and utter inability on yours, alone should warrant your refusal.

Husbands! It is now your turn. To *promote desire* is your only plan. To excite those feelings which alone can render your wishes acceptable to the partner of your love, will obviate present repugnance, and render both happy in what otherwise would be a torment to both. *Cultivate the defective faculty.* Apply those perpetual stimulants which you alone can employ, and your wife, if a true woman, will necessarily respond. This element is of right, at least always *ought* to be, comparatively dormant at marriage, and therefore requires to be *cultivated* before its full activity can reasonably be expected. This, and this *alone,* can secure your desired boon—alone can obviate the difficulty. It is not for her, but for *you,* to excite *her* to willingness. . . .

After having done all that can be done to draw out her feelings permanently, let forbearance do the rest. What but her reciprocity can render this repast agreeable to your own feelings? You are not a *man,* but a brute, if you can *insist* at her expense. Where are your higher feelings? Where is your love? Its only loss is the sacrifice of personal interest on the altar of her happiness. The wife, too, who truly loves, will most cheerfully make an equal sacrifice, and this spirit of mutual sacrifice and mutual desire to oblige, will nearly or quite control all constitutional differences, and render your union happy to both. . . .

17

FREDERICK HOLLICK

From *The Origin of Life*
1845

Frederick Hollick (1818–1900) was a major participant in the public discussion of sex at mid-century. He immigrated to the United States from Britain to join the short-lived utopian community in New Harmony, Indiana, headed by Robert Dale Owen. Although Hollick had a consultative medical practice, he earned his living primarily as a lecturer on the body and as a writer of books (see Figure 8).

Physiology of Generation in the Human Species
The Sexual Feeling, *Its origin, and use, with the consequences of unnatural, or excessive indulgence.*

THE sexual feeling, with the majority of human beings, is undoubtedly the strongest that is experienced. A proper gratification of it is, probably, productive of the highest physical enjoyment known, and is also at the foundation of the holiest and dearest moral and social delights. At the same time its ignorant and uncontrolled indulgence originates more vice, and misery, than all other causes put togther [*sic*].

This feeling cannot be suppressed, nor even subdued, to any great extent, without even greater injury than results from its unregulated license.... The idea that it is necessarily immoral, or injurious in any way, is absurd, and easily disproved both by fact and reason. Nor is it correct to speak of it as being merely an *animal,* or *sensual,* impulse; it is certainly connected with a physical function, but it is one from which results the deepest and most sacred, moral, and social interests and obligations! Sexual desire originates the holy feeling of *love,* the great tamer of mere brute passion, and the great sweetener of life.... Love, in short, refines the manners, elevates the tastes, gives a new charm to life, and is the chief bond that holds society together.

Frederick Hollick, *The Origin of Life: A Popular Treatise on the Philosophy and Physiology of Reproduction* (New York: Nafis & Cornish, 1845).

DR. HOLLICK'S
CELEBRATED WORKS ON
PHYSIOLOGY AND MEDICINE!

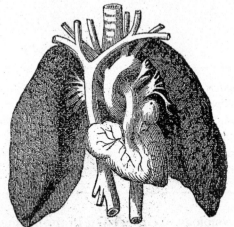

A new and uniform edition of each of the following works, illustrated with colored plates, is just published at 98 Nassau st.

These works are all *strictly scientific, moral and unobjectionable*, as well as perfectly plain, and practically useful, being written *for the People.* No others like them have ever been issued; and they contain much valuable information to be found no where else.

MARRIAGE GUIDE, or, Natural History of Generation.
            Price per copy, $1,00
MALE GENERATIVE ORGANS, in Health and Disease, from Infancy to Old Age, - - - 1,00
DISEASES OF WOMAN, at every period of Life,   1,00
MATRON'S MANUAL OF MIDWIFERY, and the Diseases of Pregnancy and Childbirth, - 1,00
ORIGIN OF LIFE, a Treatise on the Philosophy and Physiology of Reproduction in Plants and Animals, 1,00
VENEREAL DISEASES, in all their forms, a new and popular treatise on this subject is now in press, 1,00

Any or all of the above works will be sent by mail, postage free, to any part of the United States, on the receipt of *One Dollar* for each copy ordered, by the publisher,
      T. W. STRONG, 98 Nassau-st. N. Y.

Figure 8. *Magazine Advertisement for Frederick Hollick's Books, February 1855.* In the mid-nineteenth century, Hollick's books offering sexual information and advice sold well. One indication of their broad acceptance is this ad placed by T. W. Strong, a leading publisher of almanacs, children's books, and valentines, in *Yankee Notions.*

Courtesy, American Antiquarian Society.

But this love would not be born without the sexual instinct. It is not experienced till that instinct is awakened, nor when it is extinguished. . . . I consider, in short, that the sexual feeling is a legitimate and moral source of pleasure in itself, and that it is also connected with other sources of enjoyment which add greatly to the sum total of human felicity. Its development is necessary to our mental and physical perfection, and its proper gratification to our health and well being. . . .

In short, it is easy to show that the development and well being of mankind, individually and socially, depends, to a great extent, upon the due and proper gratification of our sexual feelings. We ought, therefore, to know how those feelings originate, and in what manner they should be indulged and regulated. This brings us to speak of

The Moral and Physical Causes of the Sexual Feeling

The sexual feeling, like every other physical sensation, results from a specific excitement of the nerves in certain parts of the body. In the male this part is chiefly the glans, on the end of the penis. In females it is either the external lips, the interior of the vagina, or Os Tincae[34]; but most usually the clitoris. The exciting cause is generally mechanical irritation, by copulation, or otherwise, to which persons are led by an intense desire. This desire is first produced by some unknown sympathy between the brain and sexual organs; afterwards the recollection of former pleasure increases its intensity.

The nature of this feeling cannot be described, since there is none other with which it can be compared. When fully developed it is perhaps stronger than any other, and exerts a more powerful influence, on human action. Like hunger, it originates from a physical want, which if not gratified, operates injuriously on the whole system. . . .

The mere physical desire is controlled, and regulated, by the peculiar notions of duty, or expediency, which our education has implanted within us. Desire and duty are often at variance, and it depends on their relative strength as to which shall prevail. In the poor wretch whose education has been vicious, or neglected, and whose animal desires are strong, the sense of duty is comparatively weak, and indulgence is sought at any risk. But his more fortunate brother, whose moral impressions are strong, and who has been accustomed to control his feelings, first *reflects* upon the *propriety,* and probable *consequences* of such a step; thus controlling the first impulses of passion,

---

[34]An area of the uterus at its base, lying near the cervix.

and possibly overcoming it altogether. This shows us that the proper way to remove licentiousness is, not to merely declaim against it, or enact laws for its suppression, but to cultivate, properly, the superior parts of man's nature. This operates in two ways; his mere animal impulses are counteracted, and opposed by moral ones, and are also considerably decreased in their intensity! For the cultivation of the moral and intellectual powers operates directly on the sexual organs, and diminished their action.

The immediate physical cause of the sexual feeling is, the full development of the sexual organs, from which it directly results, as hunger does from an empty stomach. The time at which this development is complete, varies, as we have seen before, according to climate, the society which young people keep, and their mode of life. By favorable circumstances it may be long retarded. In our own society it is nearly always precocious, to the great injury of human beings. In the majority of cases, directly this feeling is experienced, the desire to gratify it becomes irresistable, and either naturally or unnaturally the gratification is obtained. This leads either to open licentiousness, or to the equally great evil of solitary vice. It is an indisputable fact that there are few young persons but what fall into one or the other of these evil practices at a very early age. . . .

The best course would be to treat young persons with confidence, and act honestly towards them. As soon as they have arrived at that age when the sexual instinct is awakened, let them know its nature, the circumstances under which it may be gratified, and the consequences of improper indulgences. By thus treating them as rational beings we gain their confidence, and they will also feel a pride in meriting that confidence in future, which will act most usefully as a restraint. . . .

If this more enlighted course was adopted I have no doubt but it would diminish the evil; but still it would not entirely remove it. And for this reason, *the sexual feeling is now developed too early, before the mind is sufficiently matured to fully understand what is imparted!* This is the grand cause of the evil, and it must be removed before a sweeping reform can be accomplished. The origin of this precocious virility is to be found in the circumstances by which young people are surrounded. Years before Nature herself would develop it, the sights they have seen, the conversation they have heard, have so led them to think upon it, and so stimulated their curiosity as to call it forth. A child cannot walk out, but his eyes and ears are assailed with sights and sounds all bearing on this topic. And in many of our public prints, and in a vast deal of the current literature, it is the same. The imprudent conversation of parents even, or their incautious actions, often lead to the same result. In short, a child very soon discovers that this is the main subject of interest with nearly every person he knows, and consequently it becomes so with him at once. The mystery that surrounds it adds powerfully to that interest, and the futile attempts to keep him in ignorance only make him more determined to know.

Giving children exciting food and drink, not allowing them sufficient bodily exertion, and leaving their minds unoccupied with some innocent pursuits, are also powerful auxiliaries. A good physical education, accompanied with proper diet, makes the body muscular, disposes to active exertion, and keeps down all sexual excitement by exhausting the nervous energy in another way. In like manner, when the mind is fully and pleasantly occupied otherwise, it cannot be directed to these matters. Idleness, of body and mind, is more closely connected with licentiousness than many people suppose, particularly when accompanied by high living. . . .

The amount of sexual intercourse proper for any person cannot be stated, as it varies with individual peculiarities. There is no doubt, however, but that, as a general rule, it is practised far too much. I cannot, however, agree with some visionaries, who contend that it should only take place to a sufficient extent to propagate the species. I believe that it is also a proper and useful mode of enjoyment, under proper control, and that it brings about certain physical and moral effects which cannot be produced by any other means. To understand this we must study the connexion between the sexual organs and the rest of the system. . . .

Not only is it necessary, for the perfection of the whole human system, that the sexual organs should be fully developed, but I contend also that it is necessary for the subsequent healthy action of the system that these organs should be duly exercised. If they are not, the whole being will deteriorate. Undue continuence, in those properly organized, produces a state of nervous agitation which completely unsettles the mind, disposes the body to various diseases, and makes the disposition irritable and unhappy. It is true that cases of this kind are very rare, as most persons succumb to the temptation, and resort to some kind of gratification. Still I have known some such and others are upon record.

18

FREDERICK HOLLICK

From *The Marriage Guide*

1859

Frederick Hollick's The Origin of Life *and* The Marriage Guide *were both reprinted many times during his long life, an indication of their popularity. Although Hollick worried about sexual precocity among the young and masturbation, he was in certain ways a sexual enthusiast, advocating early marriage and regular sexual intercourse.*

Announcement

☞ OBSERVE ☚

IT has long been a matter of surprise, to reflecting people, that no book was published in the English Language, expressly relating to MARRIAGE, neither for medical men nor for popular use. The valuable and curious new discoveries which are daily being made in France, England, and Germany, are only to be found scattered through our various Medical Journals, and are but partially explained when they are found. There are but few even among medical men, therefore, who know anything about them, while the public generally are totally uninformed, and are obliged to be content with the old and absurd speculations which have been reissued over and over again for hundreds of years. . . .

On the Prevention of Conception

THIS is a subject which many persons may think not necessary to be treated upon, but there are peculiar reasons why it ought not to be passed over in silence. It has been, of late years, so much talked of, and so many unscientific works have been published, pretending to give information about it, that every one is familiar with the idea. To say that

---

Frederick Hollick, *The Marriage Guide* (New York: T. W. Strong, 1859).

there *are* means of preventing conception, is only stating what every person has already heard, or believes, and is, therefore, nothing new. . . .

There are few persons except medical men, who have any idea of the extent to which the revolting practice of Abortion is now carried, nor of the awful consequences that frequently follow from it. Every female who undergoes any of the disgusting operations practised for this purpose, does so *at the risk of her life,* and to the almost certain destruction of her health if she survives. I have had many of these miserable victims come to me afterwards for advice, and more wretched objects cannot be conceived. Some of them have been almost torn and cut to pieces, and others so injured, that their lives hung as it were by a thread. Those that take drugs for this purpose are also equally exposed to risk, and suffer in their health to an equal extent, so that their lives become a positive burthen to them. In short, this is one of the most terrible evils of the present time, and every one must earnestly desire to see it abolished, or some lesser evil take its place. Every female may be told with truth—and, indeed, every one ought to know—that there are *no safe means of procuring Abortion.* It is true that some few may undergo the ordeal in safety, but none can depend upon doing so, and the chances are ten to one that death, or the evils above referred to, will follow! . . .

I know some people will say that it is possible for some persons to avoid having a family without using *preventive* means. And so it is; but the deprivation required *will not* be undergone by the great mass, and cannot be undergone by others without the most immoral consequences. It is sheer absurdity to suppose that the promptings of Nature can be totally unheeded, except in peculiar individual cases, and illicit intercourse and vicious habits of self-indulgence would certainly follow a total deprivation of the marital right in most instances. . . .

The most obvious means of prevention are those alluded to in the Bible, as having been practised by *Onan,* and which have doubtless been in use for thousands of years.[35] If the seminal fluid be not placed within the Vagina, of course there can be no conception, and all that is required, therefore, is to cease association before the emission occurs. But, independently of the uncertainty of this being done, at least in many cases, it is not *advisable.* There is good reason to believe that, in every act of association, the presence of the male principle within the female organs is always required, even when there is no conception. It

[35]The *most obvious means of prevention* are coitus interruptus, or male withdrawal before ejaculation.

is, in all probability, more or less *absorbed* in every case, and even when it does not impregnate, it prevents irritation and exhaustion. In fact, without it, the act is merely a species of Masturbation—unsatisfactory and injurious. It is also extremely hurtful to the male, and in a way not at all suspected. When emission occurs without the female organs, it is always more incomplete and slower than when it occurs within, owing to the absence of the customary warmth and pressure, and of that peculiar influence which the organs of one sex exert upon the other. A portion of the semen, therefore, remains undischarged at the time, and escapes slowly afterwards, thus giving rise to a weakness and irritation of the Urethra and Seminal Ducts, which, in time, becomes permanent, and lays the foundation for *involuntary* losses [of semen] and final impotence.

I have known many married men much injured in this way, without being able to even conjecture what had hurt them. And I am confident that much female exhaustion and nervous irritation result in the same way. . . .

The next most general plan is the use of *Injections* after association, either for the purpose of removing the Semen, or of destroying its power.[36] For the purpose of removing it, however, they cannot always be relied upon, for sufficient will often be retained in the folds of the Vagina, to cause conception, nothwithstanding [*sic*] the injection. For the same reason, no certain dependence can be placed upon introducing any object into the Vagina before association, as a Sponge for instance. . . . There is another objection also to this, which should forbid its general use—the object introduced, of course, comes immediately before the mouth of the Womb, and then prevents the contact of that part with the male organ. Now this contact is often necessary for the production of a proper state of excitement, as formerly explained, and when it does not occur, there is simply an injurious irritation to the female, without any gratification. I have known it also cause irritation of the Meatus[37] in the male. . . .

The employment of a *covering* to the male, in the form of a thin skin tube, called a *Condom,* is of course efficacious as a preventive, but is liable to many of the above objections. . . .

Perhaps the most certain plan of *avoiding* conception is by practising association only at those times when it *cannot occur,* as explained in the article on the time when conception takes place. It is there

---

[36]The *injections* refer to Knowlton's douche method.
[37]General name for a bodily passage or canal; here most likely referring to an area of the urethra in the penis.

shown that for about one-half of each month it cannot take place, but may in the other part, so that in all cases where abstinence can be practised so long, the avoidance is easy. But even in regard to this there are some uncertainties, as already shown, owing to the irregularity of the functions in some females, though this does not effect many, and therefore the plan appears on the whole the most feasible. It has also the great advantage of not being in any way positively hurtful to either, though it unfortunately limits the association to that period when the female *least desires it,* which is an evil, and shows that nature does not favor prevention in any way, but on the contrary favors Reproduction.[38]

Those females who think they can escape being impregnated simply by avoiding all excitement, and pleasurable feeling, are more deceived than those who rely on any of the other modes, as former explanations have shown. . . .

[38]Hollick here advocated what came to be called "the rhythm method" of birth control in the twentieth century; however, he and others in his day relied on a faulty connection of the time of ovulation with menstruation.

The Fourth Framework:
Sex at the Center of Life

19

THOMAS L. NICHOLS, M.D.

From *Esoteric Anthropology*

1854

Thomas Low Nichols (1815–1901) and Mary Gove (1810–1884) were instrumental in creating the fourth framework, which placed sex at the center of life. After a varied career as a journalist and writer of fiction, Nichols met Gove in 1847. With their marriage in 1848, Nichols entered

T. L. Nichols, M.D., *Esoteric Anthropology: A Comprehensive and Confidential Treatise on the Structure, Functions, Passional Attractions and Perversions, True and False Physical and Social Conditions, and the Most Intimate Relations of Men and Women* (New York: Published by the author, at his Reform Bookstore, No. 65 Walker Street, 1854).

medical school in order to join his wife in her successful career in water cure. Upon his graduation, the two collaborated in writing books, founding a journal, and establishing schools. Gove likely served as coauthor of Esoteric Anthropology, *for she advocated many of its Grahamite ideas, such as the separation of the nerves of organic life and those of animal life. The book is an unusual work of moral physiology in the following ways. In discussions of lovemaking, it uses prose generally reserved for fiction. Its physiological sections use words precisely and offer graphic descriptions. It names and describes birth control techniques, including the syringe, the sponge, and the condom. Although condemning abortion as a sin against nature, the book discusses it clearly and gives alternative procedures. It addresses homosexuality in men and women.*

To the Reader

... This is no book for the center-table, the library shelf, or the counter of a bookstore. As its name imports, it is a *private treatise* on the most interesting and important subjects. It is of the nature of A STRICTLY CONFIDENTIAL PROFESSIONAL CONSULTATION BETWEEN PHYSICIAN AND PATIENT, in which the latter wishes to know all that can be of use to him, and all that the former is able and willing to teach. It is such a book as I wish to put into the hands of every man and every woman—yes, and every child wise enough to profit by its teachings—*and no others....*

... Every man who purifies and invigorates his own life, does something for the world. Every woman who lives in the conditions of health, and avoids the causes of disease, helps the race; and if such persons combine their purified and invigorated lives in healthy offspring, they do a noble work for the redemption of universal humanity....

Happiness, enjoyment, pleasure, or whatever word may express to us the natural and harmonious action and gratification of the human passions, appears to be the single end or final cause of creation. We are unable to conceive of any other motive. Every faculty is for use, every organ to perform its function, and every function gives, or in some way contributes, to enjoyment....

Function of Generation

THE generative function has for its special use the continuation of the species; and it is intimately connected with the highest processes of both the systems of organic and animal life. There is no action of the body, and no power of the soul, which does not enter into the complicated and beautiful process by which humanity exists, and new beings are created. For the performance of this great function, we have a peculiar power or passion of the soul; a separate organ in the brain; nerves of exquisite sensation, voluntary and involuntary nerves of motion, with their muscular apparatus; and the most complex organs of innervation, circulation, nutrition, and secretion, connected with the system of organic life. Through all her works, nature has taken peculiar care of this function, often raised it above all others, and sacrificed all individual interests to the general welfare. . . .

It is remarkable, that the parts of plants devoted to the sexual function, are those we most prize for their beauty and fragrance. It is the flower of the plant which contains the generative organs. The center of the flower—the home of beauty, and fragrance, and sweetness—is the nuptial couch, the bower of love, sacred to the passionate mysteries of vegetable procreation. In the center of this bridal chamber is the pistil, or female organ; its tube corresponds to the vagina, and below it is the ovary, where the egg is formed and fecundated. This is done by one or more stamens which surround the pistil, and which have the power of secreting the spermatic fluid, which, in the form of pollen, falls upon the anther of the pistol. The stamen corresponds to the testicles and penis of the higher male animals. . . .

. . . When the period of puberty has fully arrived, there comes a wonderful change over the whole being. No after change, till death itself comes, is so rapid and important. Soul and body expand with new powers and new feelings. The boy finds a beard sprouting on his chin, and hair also springing on the pubes. His neck increases in size by the expansion of the cerebellum behind, and the larynx in front. With the expansion of the larynx, his voice sinks a full octave in depth. He finds his penis growing to what seems to him an extraordinary size. The testicles also increase. He has frequent erections; and his mind is filled with ideas of voluptuousness. His ideas of women are not so entirely romantic as before; still it is left for his dreams to give him to the full power of his senses. Fortunate is the youth whose love for some adorable woman chastens the ardor of these fancies, and prevents the waste of this new-found life!

Puberty, in the girl, brings no less remarkable changes. There is no beard upon the face, but a luxuriant growth of hair begins to cover the mons veneris. The larynx does not expand, nor the voice deepen, but the cerebellum, though always smaller than in the male, increases in size, and the form expands into the full mold of womanly beauty. The whole pelvis enlarges, giving breadth to the hips, and a graceful swing to the carriage. The mammary glands enlarge, producing in all healthily developed girls, the bosom of ravishing voluptuousness—the bosom which sculptors and painters are never tired of showing us, but which women commonly conceal, unless fashion compels the exposure. But the most striking change that takes place when the girl becomes a woman, is the commencement of a monthly discharge from the uterus, through the vagina, coincident with and dependent upon the ripening of the germs in the ovaries.

Both sexes are now apparently fitted for the performance of the sexual function. In the male, the testicles have secreted the spermatic fluid, and elaborated its vital part, the living spermatozoa; the seminal vesicles are filled with this fluid, ready to be discharged. In the female, the ovaries have begun to bring forth the ova, which contains the germs, which only require the presence of the spermatic fluid, to be developed into perfect human beings. . . .

The passion of love, as it reigns in the soul of man, harmonizing and energizing his animal and organic systems, has three general modes of expression.

1. It gives a feeling of regard for the whole opposite sex. It inspires in man a gallant respect for woman; in woman, a tender regard for man.

2. In a circumscribed sphere, it is social in its character and action. A man has for the women of his acquaintance, whom he meets in society, and with whom he is on terms of kindly familiarity, a very different feeling from any he entertains toward the other sex. . . .

3. Personal love, beginning with a spiritual attraction, becoming voluptuous desire, and seeking its ultimate expression in sexual union. This is the last, fullest, and most perfect action of the amative passion; that which consummates the life and happiness of the individual, and governs the destiny of the race. . . .

What the human soul demands for every passion and every function, is freedom; liberty of thought, liberty of desire, liberty of expression and action. . . .

Men who have romantic fancies in boyhood and early youth; violent love-fits in early manhood, which give place to calmer, stronger, and more enduring loves, in their maturity; these may be exclusive, or monogamic, or, in more varied and expansive natures, may be consistent with subordinate affections, desires, and gratifications. . . .

Marriage, in a higher and purer sense, is the real union of two persons in mutual love; and adultery is, perhaps, best defined as any gratification of mere lust, or the sensual nature, without the sanctification of a true love. According to these definitions, a true marriage may be what the laws call adultery, while the real adultery is an unloving marriage. . . .

In animals where there is but one gestation in a year, there is usually but one period of heat; but while the periods of gestation and lactation extend over nearly two years in the human female, when these are at an end, she regularly, every month, throws off an ovum, marked by the menstrual discharge; and, of course, is every month prepared to receive the sexual embrace. It seems to be fairly inferable, that once a month is the natural period in which a woman requires sexual union; and it may be doubted whether any greater frequency is not a violation of natural law. . . .

Man differs very materially from woman in the exercise of the procreative function. From the age of puberty, the action of the testis is uninterrupted. I can find no hint of periodicity, unless it has been created by habit. Whatever restraints he may have, must be moral: for they are not physical, like woman's. And while, in woman, the production of ova ceases at from forty-five to fifty, the activity of the organs in man continues, and he is capable of generating until a late period of life, and in some cases when more than a century old. Man has no function corresponding in periodicity to menstruation; no diversions of the vital forces engaged in this function, like those of pregnancy and lactation. . . .

. . . If a woman has any right in this world, it is the right to herself; and if there is any thing in this world she has a right to decide, it is who shall be the father of her children. She has an equal right to decide whether she will have children, and to choose the time for having them.

This is a law of nature, respected throughout the animal kingdom. The female everywhere refuses sexual union with the male, except at the appointed season; and compulsion at any time, and especially during pregnancy, can not be called beastly, for it would be a libel on the brutes.

But what are men to do! I really can not answer. They must do the best they can. If I have correctly interpreted nature so far, we have nothing to do but to search still further for the truth. Nature has not provided for one sex at the expense of the other. . . .

The expressions of love antecedent to, and connected with its ultimation, are varied and beautiful, involving the whole being. Love gives light, and a trembling suffusion to the eye, a soft, tremulous tenderness to the voice, a sweet sadness to the demeanor, or a deep joyousness; a certain warmth and voluptuousness presides over the movements of the body; blushes come often to the cheeks, and the eyes are cast down with consciousness; the heart swells, and beats tumultuously; there is a radiant idealization of the beloved object, who seems clothed with every perfection; a new delight pervades the sense of feeling, which is more than any other the organ of this passion; every touch, even of the hem of the garment, is a deep pleasure; the hands clasp each other with a thrill of delight; the lips cling together in dewy kisses of inexpressible rapture; the bolder hands of man wander over the ravishing beauties of woman; he clasps her waist, he presses her soft bosom, and in a tumult of delirious ecstasy, each finds the central point of attraction and of pleasure, which increases until it is completed in the sexual orgasm—the most exquisite enjoyment of which the human senses are capable.

It has been asked whether the male or female enjoyed most the ultimation of love. I have no doubt, that in a healthy condition, the pleasure of the female is longer continued, more frequently repeated, and more exquisite than that of the male; and that it is in this way that she is compensated for her long periods of deprivation; as she also is by the pleasures of maternity, of which man has little conception.

There are a few practical observations, which may be properly made here, connected with the physiology of the sexual congress as given above. The organs of generation, in both sexes, are excited and stimulated by idleness, luxury, and every form of voluptuous beauty. Where it is desirable to avoid such excitement, all these must be guarded against. Passionate poetry and romances, warm pictures, dancing, especially the dancing of the stage, the fashionable display of female arms and bosoms, all fond toyings, and personal freedoms between the sexes, must be avoided by those with whom chastity is a necessity of age or circumstance. The lips are supplied with nerves of sensation from the cerebellum; and the kisses of the lips are sacred to love. The bosom is also supplied with nerves from the same source, and it is in the most direct and intimate sympathy with the female generative organs. A woman of sensibility, who would preserve her chastity, must guard her bosom well.

But the best safeguard against one passion, is to arouse another, and, if possible, many others. Friendship is often a safeguard against love; even the friendship of young persons of opposite sexes. . . . Business, study, active exercises, amusement, ambition, reverence, a constant occupation of mind and body, divert the vital forces into so many channels, that the system feels no pressing wants in this direction, and men live in the bustle of active life, for months and even years, without amative wants.

Women govern themselves much more easily than men. With great numbers, continence is no virtue, for they have not the least attraction for sexual connection, nor are they capable of sexual enjoyment. This is, indeed, a diseased condition, hereditary or acquired; but it is common to an incredible degree. But even with women of passionate natures, who are capable of the most ardent love, and the fullest enjoyment, certain conditions are necessary to the awakening of sexual desire. They must love, and be beloved. Love must begin in the soul as a sentiment, come down into the heart as a passion, before it can descend into the body as a desire. Such a woman will be continent without the least difficulty, so long as she does not love; but when she loves a man, she gives herself to him, soul and body. Happy the man who can inspire and respond to such a love! Happy the child born of such a union! Happy the human race, when there shall be no others! . . .

Of Frequency of Sexual Indulgence

I have given what I believe to be the natural law of the generative function; but we are so far from a natural condition, that I scarcely expect any one to follow it. Thousands of men so "run to seed," as to insist on having sexual intercourse daily, and in some cases several times a day. I have known men who indulged morning, noon, and night. But I have also known men to murder, in this way, three or four wives, in rapid succession; and the world is full of victims of this inordinate lust. It is, however, but fair to say, that the victims are not all of one sex. Many a pale, thin, weak-backed man is suffering from gratifying the morbid desires of a strong, passionate, diseased woman. When women are diseased in this way, they go further than is possible with men. . . . A woman, who loses no semen, and simply expends a certain amount of nervous force, will have six or seven orgasms in rapid succession, each seeming to be more violent and ecstatic than the last. These may be accompanied with screams, bitings, spasms, and end in a faint languor, that will last for many hours. . . .

It is my opinion that no one, male or female, ought to average more than once a week. If within a few days after the menstrual period, this amount of indulgence was had, and for the rest of the month refrained from, it would be nearer to a natural condition.

Of Certain Unnatural Manifestations

Among the crimes punished with death under the Mosaic law, were bestiality, sodomy, and incest. All are more or less unnatural, but I see no good reason for continuing the penalty, or for making them in any way the subjects of human retribution. Under the Mosaic dispensation there were, I believe, fourteen offenses punished with death. Many of these are not now reckoned offenses, and for most of the others the punishment is modified. I see no reason for punishing a man for an act which begins and ends with himself, or with a consenting party. Moreover, such laws are useless, as not one case in a thousand, from its very nature, can ever be brought to justice.

Amativeness, excited by false modes of living, and made rampant by social repressions, runs into many morbid expressions. Of these, masturbation, or self-pollution, is the most common and the most destructive. It prevails to about an equal extent in both sexes, and probably not more than one person in ten, of either sex, entirely escapes it. Many of the noblest, loveliest, and purest are wrecked by this habit, the result of parental sensuality and unnatural modes of life.

Sodomy, or the intercourse of one male with another, has been practiced from the remotest ages, and is still so common in Eastern and tropical countries, as not to excite remark. It is also practiced among prisoners, soldiers, and sailors, all of whom are subject to false conditions. It also occurs from the mere choice of a morbid lust, with men who have every opportunity for gratification with the other sex. This was so common in classic times, that Voltaire has thought it necessary to defend Solon, Plutarch, and even Socrates, from the charge of having recommended or defended it. It is even called Socratic love, as a similar passion of females for each other, and their mutual gratification of each other's desires is called Sapphic love, from Sappho, who has celebrated this not unfrequent perversion in some pretty and passionate verses.

Filthy as this practice is in one case, and false as it is in both, it is probably less hurtful than the far more common practice of solitary vice. . . .

Can One Love Two or More Persons at Once?

This is simply a question of capacity. One man is stronger than another: one has far greater versatility. A man finds himself capable of loving five or six children, and several friends. But how is it, in point of fact? I have seen women who assured me that they had no power to love but one man at a time, though capable of a succession of amours. Others believe that one love is enough for a lifetime. There are others who seem to love two, three, or even more, with various degrees of passion, but all amatively.... Over three quarters of the world polygamy is tolerated, and more or less practiced. It is absurd to suppose that no man ever loves more than one wife; as absurd as to suppose that European and American women, as long as they love their husbands, can love nobody else. A belief in this doctrine is the basis of much jealousy and domestic tyranny.... The monogamic idea is therefore the parent of jealousy and all its tyrannies.

What Is Virtue?

... In point of fact, men and women are not on equal terms, in the present form of marriage. Women have no pecuniary independence, nor, except in rare cases, the means of acquiring it. For the most part they are dependent parasites: and though the cares of a family and the bearing of children may be equal to any exertions of the husband, still the woman, by custom and law, is made dependent upon man for support. As long as a woman lives in this condition of acknowledged dependence, she must conform to her husband's wishes, and can not exercise the rights of a sovereign individual.

A woman has, naturally, the supreme right of choosing who shall be the father of her child; but she can have no right to receive the support of one man, while she bears a child to another, except by consent. A woman is bound, therefore, to be true to her marriage relation, while the relation exists....

The duties of a husband to his wife must be reciprocal just so far as their relations are equilibrated. In some respects they strikingly differ. During a large portion of the time, a child-bearing woman is not in a condition to allow sexual intercourse. A woman has usually no such excuse for infidelity.... With the man, the physical consequences terminate with the act; with the woman, they may remain for months and years. These are evidently real differences, which must modify our ideas of duty and criminality, in and out of the marriage relation, and the civilized notions in this respect are not entirely destitute of foundation. . . .

The world is changing its ideas on these subjects. There is an influx of light from the spiritual world, and this light brings us knowledge, freedom, and purity. Thousands of couples live together as friends, who once believed themselves to be married—giving each other freedom and protection; thousands more, caring less for the conservative world, or having more violent repulsions, break the bonds and separate; and divorces are becoming more frequent and easier to procure. . . .

Is Love Enduring?

. . . Can we say, then, of any love that it will last forever, or even for ten years? We believe it will—we always believe this; but in the light of observation and experience, can we *promise it?* The most any one can safely promise is to be true to himself, and true to his love while it continues. He can do no more. . . .

As love is the basis, the condition, the reality of marriage, it follows that where love ends, marriage ends. Marriage without love is a sham and a mockery. . . .

That two young persons, who have flirted, and danced, and simpered, and dawdled through a fashionable courtship, and then stood up before a parson, in white gloves, satin, and orange flowers,[39] should be compelled to bore, and torment, and torture each other and every body about them, till one dies, or is sent to State prison, is a refinement of cruelty that only our absurd civilization could be guilty of. I truly believe, that in a social, moral, and religious point of view, if every marriage not founded on the true basis of mutual love were broken up, the world would be immeasurably the gainer. . . .

Continuance of Sexual Desire

. . . Many persons believe that the sole object and only justifiable motive to sexual indulgence, is the begetting of children, and that the act is sinful under all other circumstances. There are many difficulties

---

[39] *Orange flowers* were traditional elements in a wedding bouquet, for in the "language of flowers" they suggested purity and love. The statement associated with them by the late nineteenth century was "Your purity equals your loveliness."

attending this theory. The passion of love, and its sentimental enjoyments, the influence it has upon the character, the strength of the
attraction for sexual union, and the exquisite and delicious pleasure it
brings, in a healthy state, to both sexes, all point to other uses and
ends than those of procreation. If this were the only use of sexual connection, why should the passionate desire for, and complete enjoyment of it, continue, when the generative power has ceased? A woman
ceases to be capable of bearing children at forty-five to fifty-five. There
comes then what is called "the turn of life." The ovaries cease to produce germs—there is no longer any appearance of the menses; but
the power to love remains in its full force and ardor, and the desire
and capacity for sexual pleasure.

20

THOMAS L. NICHOLS AND
MARY S. GOVE NICHOLS

From *Marriage*

1854

In Marriage, *Nichols and Gove's openly collaborative book, the authors
treated free love explicitly, each approaching the topic from a different
position. Nichols allowed sex with multiple partners. Gove stood for the
right of divorce and remarriage. Immigrating to England at the outset of
the Civil War, Nichols and Gove left behind a complex heritage that
would resonate through the decades to come.*

What Will Become of the Children?

. . . Freedom in love will put an end to all involuntary, compulsory, and
repugnant maternity. When women are set free from the domestic
servitude of marriage; when they sustain themselves in independence

T. L. Nichols and Mary S. Gove Nichols, *Marriage: Its History, Character, and Results; Its
Sanctities, and Its Profanities; Its Science and Its Facts* (Cincinnati, Ohio: Valentine
Nicholson & Company, 1854).

by their own industry;—no man will have the power to force them to
have children contrary to their own desires. The hundreds of thousands of miserable beings that now perish in infancy *will not be born.*
When women have children, it will be because they wish to have
them; and the maternal instinct of every female animal prompts her to
provide for her offspring.

The children, born in the attraction and passion of a mutual love,
will be strong and healthy; and thus freedom will soon give vigor to
the race.

When men are drawn by the attraction of beauty, grace, elegance;
and women are free to follow their natural attraction for strength,
courage, and every manly and noble quality,—the constant tendency
will be toward the improvement of the race. A few generations of freedom would change the whole aspect of society. Hereditary diseases
and deformities would be eradicated. Every child would be the result
of the highest love and the best conditions of which its parents at the
time were capable.

But these children, how are they to be supported, cared for, and
educated?

When women are free, and self-sustaining, they will be prompted
by the most universal instinct of nature, to provide for all the children
they have, or to have no children for whom they cannot provide. This
instinct being weaker in man, he is more reckless in the gratification
of his passions; and this is the reason why so many children are now
unprovided for, and why this whole affair of maternity should be
under woman's control. To her who bears its burdens, it properly
belongs. . . .

. . . We need not doubt that fathers, when they are no longer in the
false position of despots and masters, will obey the instincts of nature,
and the promptings of honor and parental love.

The beautiful, healthful, and happy children, who are born from
unions of mutual love, of independent, self-relying, self-sustaining
women, are not likely to be a burthen[40] to any society, or an onerous
charge to any State. Everywhere such children will be a pride and a
blessing. . . .

What Is Morality?

IT is time for us to examine, and settle this question. If I say, morality
is a conformity to the law of God, the most "orthodox" will not dispute

---

[40]A varient of burden, meaning load or responsibility.

the assertion. I accept the definition fully — I insist upon it. The law of God is impressed upon the constitution of every being, and belongs to its organization. The use of every faculty, possessed by any being, the gratification of every instinctive desire, the exercise of every power, the enjoyment of every happiness, is the fullest possible conformity of that being to the law of God.

No one will dispute this, if asserted of the lower animals. We never think of their instinctive acts being immoral.

I assert the same of man. He has no sense, faculty or passion that was not made for use, and whose use does not contribute to his happiness. These faculties are liable to perversion and disease. These diseases arise chiefly from repressions, or efforts to control, thwart, or suppress them. Acting in freedom, their tendency is to harmony. Confined, dammed up, tabooed, they break out into injurious excesses and diseased manifestations, like the gluttony of those who have been starved, or the riotous saturnalia of slaves.

Man's morality, his most perfect conformity to the law of God, is his fullest and most harmonious exercise of all his natural faculties, and the complete gratification of all his natural desires. No talent is to be buried in a napkin; no organ is to be sacrificed or perverted from its natural use and enjoyment. If we fail to develop one faculty, or to satisfy one inborn desire of our natures, we fail in our duty to God, in our conformity to nature, in justice to ourselves, and bring discordance into the universal harmony.

The rigid moralist, according to the civilized standard, is therefore the most immoral of beings; he is one who lives in a continual violation of the laws of God, as they are impressed upon his own mental and physical organization. . . .

The morality of nature is pure, holy, universal, harmonious, and produces the greatest happiness every being is capable of enjoying. The moralism of civilization is obscene, impious, partial, discordant, and produces everywhere disease of body and misery of soul, plunging man into a hideous concatenation of discord and crime.

It is my right, it is my highest duty, to use every organ, every sense, every faculty which God has given me. In the exercise and use of all these faculties, in the performance of every natural function of my life, I find the greatest possible pleasure, and the most complete and perfect happiness of which my nature is capable. This is true morality; this only is true virtue; this is a perfect conformity to the will of God. When all men and women are developed up to this thought and life, then will the will of God be done on earth as it is in heaven. . . .

2

Controversy and Commerce

Phase 1: The 1840s

21

MADAME RESTELL

Advertisements

March 2, 1842

---

*Madame Restell was the business name of Ann Trow Lohman (1811–
1878), the most famous abortionist in New York City. An emigrant from
England, she began her work in the late 1830s and, aided by Charles
Lohman, her printer husband, advertised her services openly in the
penny press. The illustration opposite shows one such advertisement.*

Advertisements, Madame Restell, *New York Herald,* March 2, 1842. Courtesy, American
Antiquarian Society.

MADAME RESTELL,

FEMALE PHYSICIAN, Office and residence 148 Green wich street, (between Cortlandt and Liberty streets,) where she can be consulted with the strictest confidence on all complaints incident to the female frame

Madame Restell's experience and knowledge in the treatment of obstinate cases of female irregularity, stoppage or suppression, &c, is such as to require but a few days for certain relief and perfect recovery. Ladies desiring proper medical attendance during confinement or other indisposition, will be accommodated during such time with private and respectable board. "Preventive Powders" for married ladies whose delicate or precarious health forbids a too rapid increase of family, will be sent by mail to any part of the United States. Price $5 a package. All letters (post paid) addressed to 'box 868, N. Y. city,' will be received.

Boston Office No. 7 Essex st.

N. B.—Madame Restell would inform ladies residing out of the city, whose health would not admit of travelling, that she would devote her personal attendance upon them in any part of the United States within reasonable distance,

f18 d&w1m*

COUNTERFEIT. FEMALE MONTHLY PILLS.

OWING to the celebrity, efficacy and invariable success of Madame Restell's Female Monthly Pills in all cases of irregularity, suppression, or stoppage of those functions of nature upon which the health of every female depends, since their introduction into the United States, now about four years, counterfeits and imitations are continually attempted to be palmed off for the genuine. Cheap common pills are purchased at twelve cents a box, put up in different boxes, and called "Female Monthly Pills," with the object of selling, if possible, at one dollar. Females are therefore cautioned against these attempts to impose upon them. It is sufficient here to state that all Female Monthly Pills are counterfeits, except those sold at Madame Restell's Principal Office, 148 Greenwich st. New York, and No. 7 Essex street, Boston. Price $1.

Madame Restell's signature is written on the cover of each box.

N. B. The married, under some circumstances, must abstain from their use for reasons contained in the directions.

f18 d&w1m*

22

From *The Magdalen Report*

1831

---

*Although prostitution was a big business in New York, with an estimated
200 brothels and uncounted houses of assignation, before the 1830s it
was seldom discussed openly in print. In 1831, John R. McDowall, a
young urban missionary brought to the city by the American Tract Society, issued the* Magdalen Report, *which introduced information about
the trade to the public and called for reform. McDowall's primary concern was for the young men of the city whose lives and souls he believed
were endangered by prostitutes (whose numbers he overestimated). His
report caused a storm of protest, especially among those who felt it was
indelicate and that it endangered youth by providing a guide to brothel
life. Evangelical women took up McDowall's cause, however, forming the
New York Female Moral Reform Society and issuing their own* Advocate
for Moral Reform, *which offered a critique of contemporary sexual morals
and society's toleration of male lechery.*

The extent of prostitution in this city, as shown by facts already developed during our labors, and the alarming increase of the unhappy victims of seduction among us, of which we have attained the most
demonstrative evidence, so far exceed all our own previous calcula-
tions, that we are prepared to anticipate scepticism and incredulity in
others. Indeed enough is in our possession to cause a thrill of horror
to be felt by every virtuous man and woman in the community, such
as was never produced by any expose of vice which has ever met the
public eye. Did not prudence and delicacy forbid the disgusting detail
of what has been brought to our knowledge thus early in the history
of this Society, every parent would tremble for the safety of his sons
as well as his daughters, and we could a tale disclose which would
cause the blood to "chill within the veins, and each particular hair to
stand erect, like quills upon the fretted porcupine." But we shall forbear, and only set forth those general facts which plead for the neces-

---

*The Magdalen Report: First Annual Report of the Executive Committee of the New-York
Magdalen Society* (New York: printed for the publishers, 1831).

sity of extensive and efficient efforts, in behalf of those unhappy females, for whose reformation and salvation the New-York Magdalen Society is engaged.

First then we would present the fact, that we have satisfactorily ascertained that the number of females in this city, who abandon themselves to prostitution is not less than TEN THOUSAND!! The data on which this estimate is founded are, first, the opinion of the Alderman, whose experience and observation for several years past, as Commissioner at Bellevue,[1] enabled him to judge very accurately, and from whom we learned in the commencement of our labors, what we then thought improbable, that there were *ten thousand harlots in this city.*" But although we then judged that the number was overrated, we are driven to the painful admission, that his estimate was just, from our own observation in the partial census we have attempted.

We have the names, street and number of the houses of ill-fame in this city, notoriously inhabited by abandoned women; and also the houses of assignation where daily and nightly the pollution of girls and women of all ages and colors, married and single, is habitually committed. Many of these sinks of iniquity are in respectable neighborhoods, disguised under the mask of boarding houses, dressmakers, milliners, stores and shops of various kinds. Some of them are large and elegant houses, provided with costly furniture, and have brass and silver plates on the doors, on which are engraved the real or fictitious names of the occupants.

These haunts of iniquity have been discovered partly by the aid of the Police officers, partly by the girls and women who have been rescued from pollution by the Asylum,[2] and partly by the vigilance of persons, male and female, employed by the Society. By these means we have arrived at very many of the secrets of these nests of abomination, the number of lewd women who reside or resort to each, the arts and intrigues by which the victims of seduction are procured, as well as the *names* of scores of the men and boys who are the seducers of the innocent, or the companions of the polluted. Hence our opportunity of judging of the extent of prostitution in the city, is now by no means limited, and we are satisfied we do not exaggerate when we repeat, that there are now *ten thousand* girls and women, in the city of

[1]A complex of three institutions: a penitentiary, an almshouse (poor house), and a hospital. Prostitutes would likely have been found in all three.
[2]Most likely the "House of Refuge" in New York City, run by the Magdalen Society under McDowall's leadership.

New-York, who live by public and promiscuous prostitution. Besides these we have the clearest evidence that there are hundreds of private harlots and kept misses, many of whom keep up a show of industry as domestics, seamstresses, nurses, &c., in the most respectable families, and throng the houses of assignation every night. Although we have no means of ascertaining the number of these, yet enough has been learned from the facts already developed to convince us that the aggregate of these is alarmingly great, perhaps little behind the proportion of the city of London, whose police reports assert, on the authority of accurate researches, that the number of private prostitutes in that city, is fully equal to the number of public harlots. This is a most appalling picture of moral degradation, and we forbear to dwell upon so painful and mortifying conclusions as those to which this view of the subject would impel us. . . .

Some of these, it is revolting to human nature to relate, are devoted to prostitution thus early in life by their own *mothers,* either in their own houses kept as brothels, or placed, by these unnatural monsters in female form, in the houses kept by others.

Besides these, many of them are the daughters of the wealthy, respectable and pious citizens of our own and other states, seduced from their homes by the villains who infest the community, preying upon female innocence, and succeeding in their diabolical purpose, either by promises of marriage; or, after deceiving them into a brothel, by the commission of rape; often first depriving the victims of their lust, of their reason, by stupefying drugs kept in these dens of iniquity for the purpose. Individual cases of each of these descriptions are known to the Society, in which the unhappy girl has been kept imprisoned for weeks, until all hope of escape from infamy was lost, and she at last gave herself up to intemperance and crime.

Among these are very many daughters of poor parents, and especially widowed mothers, whose necessities compelled them to seek employment as domestics. For such, especially the young and inexperienced, the keepers of these brothels are eagerly seeking in the character of procuresses, and soon after hiring them as servants, they are sent into a room with some man, or rather monster in human shape, and compelled to submit to his vile purpose, for which the procuress is liberally paid. The poor girl now finds herself ruined, and is presently seduced to consent to a life of infamy, by the promise of plenty of money, fine clothes, &c., and all is lost. Numbers of these cases have already come under our observation, in which many women were thus the active agents in effecting the ruin of the young and unwary of their own sex.

Great numbers of them have been married to drunken husbands, brought to this city, far from their homes and friends, and here abandoned with one or more children, perhaps shockingly diseased, and left to starve, or provide for themselves. Without friends, money, or character, they are soon found by some of those who prowl about for such prey, their children die from neglect or cruelty, or perhaps are sent to the Alms House,[3] while the mothers give themselves up to guilt and infamy.

But we will not affect to conceal that hundreds, perhaps thousands of them, are the daughters of the ignorant, depraved and vicious part of our population, trained up without culture of any kind, amidst the contagion of evil example, and enter upon a life of prostitution for the gratification of their unbridled passions, and become harlots altogether by choice. These have a short career, generally dying of the effects of intemperance and pollution soon after entering upon this road to ruin. . . .

It is a lamentable fact that men are the original cause of the evil complained of; yet it is but too true that women take their revenge an hundred fold. Seductions of females amongst us are often attended with peculiar aggravations, and the abandoned of both sexes are reciprocally tempters of the virtuous. But it is clearly ascertained that bad women multiply the seduction of heedless youth, more rapidly than bad men seduce modest women. A few of these courtesans suffice to corrupt whole cities, and there can be no doubt that some insinuating prostitutes have initiated more young men into these destructive ways, than the most abandoned rakes have debauched virgins during their whole lives. So though the latter deserve execration and great severity, yet the grand effort of those who would promote reformation, should be directed to arresting, and if possible reclaiming, those wretched females, who are the pest and nuisance of society, though equally the objects of our compassion and abhorrence.

---

[3] The poor house at Bellevue.

23

SUNDAY FLASH

Lives of the Nymphs, No. 11: Amanda Green
October 17, 1841

The creation of male sporting life went hand in hand with commercial developments, including weekly papers collectively called the flash press, that took as a central feature the portrayal of brothel life. These papers began in 1841 in New York, taking such titles as the Sunday Flash, *the* Whip, *and the* Rake. *This story of the seduction of Amanda Green appeared in an early number of the first sporting paper and was named in the obscenity indictment of its publishers, William Joseph Snelling, George Wooldridge, and George Wilkes. In this and other selections from the flash papers, there are many spelling and grammatical errors, likely caused by the speed and carelessness of authors and printers.*

This celebrated nymph was born in this city, though what particular street[,] lane, or alley, or what house in such street, lane or alley, had the honor of producing her, we cannot pretend to say. She was born somewhere in the North side of town, her mother was a mantua-maker,[4] and through industry and a good run of custom, pretty well to do is the world [*sic*]. At the age of six, Amanda was sent to school and achieved that invaluable accomplishment possessed by so few cyprians[5] in this city, of being able to read. In due time, she also learned to write and cypher,[6] and having now gained the *ne plus ultra*[7] of her literary hopes, she left school and assisted her mother in her business. By-and-by, she grew up, and right pretty did she grow too and many a grocer's clerk and amorous shopboy, would find his mouth water and his heart beat as she went about the neighborhood on errands, and

---

[4]A dressmaker.
[5]*Cyprians* is a term used in the nineteenth century for prostitutes.
[6]To perform arithmetic.
[7]*Ne plus ultra* means the ultimate or highest.

"Lives of the Nymphs, No. 11: Amanda Green," *Sunday Flash* 1, no. 11 (Oct. 17, 1841): 3.

many a liquorish old goat and salacious young one, would wear out his ineffectual leather in following her about when business drew her far from home. But Amanda had not yet felt the throb of passion in a high degree, or if she had, had the discretion to master it, for the only answers for which she returned to these unlawful solicitations were "Git along you sassy good for nothin feller, I can find my way home by myself," and so she battled off the annoyance.

One evening, a dress had been finished for a lady in Hudson Street and Amanda was to take it home. It was snowing at the time, and the distance was great, yet the dress must be carried. Unwillingly our heroine set out, performed her errand and on her return home, was about crossing Hudson Street when the jingle of a fast approaching sleigh warned her to stand back. The person driving, seeing a pretty female on the road, stopped the sleigh and apologizing for endangering her safety begged her to allow him to drive her home as a recompense. This Amanda refused and was about shipping to the other side, when the gentleman sprang out, clasped her in his arms, lifted her in, whistled to his horse and the next moment was flying along like mad; her complaints drowned by the clatter of the bells, and pursuit rendered fruitless by the speed at which they dashed over the ground. Giving his horse its head, the kidnapper took no notice of his course and only appeared anxious to convince Amanda of his kind intentions toward her; and to that end clasped her again and again in his arms and pressed upon her unwilling (so says Amanda) lips, a thousand kisses. After the proper quantum of struggling and crying, she became subdued and reposed unresistingly in his arms—perhaps she found a comfort in his bear's-skin coat, for to say the truth the night was very cold.

At length, the horse, who appeared to understand his part as well as his master dashed up a long avenue and stopped at the gate of a very neat chateau, which from a ruddy light that shone through the windows, promised comfortable refuge from the storm. Lifting her in his arms like a child, though Amanda was by no means a chicken, the stalwart stranger bore her into a handsomely furnished room, where a most cheerful hickory fire was blazing high up in the chimney. Setting her down near it in a luxurious chair, he relieved her of her snow-burdened bonnet and shawl, and leaving the room a moment, returned with his outer garments also cast off. Finding herself housed in a strange place, with no prospect of getting home, another fit of crying came on, but this the assiduous stranger, who we shall now call

Chambers, silenced, and persuaded her to drink a glass of hot negus,[8] which was just then brought in the room by a stunted black waiter of about three feet high, who was at the same time one of the ugliest specimens of dingy humanity that Amanda had ever befeld. A hot and sumptuous supger followed this, and exhilerated by the share of a bottle of champaigne, she submitted without further opposition to his advances and toward the last returned them with interest. The sequel can be easily seen. At the crowing of the cock she was no more a maid. The next morning Amanda felt no inclination to return home and in accordance with her own and her lover's feelings, she resolved to abide with him for a time.

Far and near, and high and low, was she sought after, but no tidings heard, and at the end of a month, she was accounted by her friends as dead, and no further search made for her. Amanda remained at the Chateau some three months, when she discovered by a letter that Chambers was unfaithful to her, and sick at heart at the depravity of the man who owed her constancy, if nothing else, she left his establishment, returned to her mother, told her story and asked forgiveness. The softhearted parent, who looked upon her child as one risen from the grave, forgave her at once and with a warning to stead her for the future, took her to her bosom.

For six months did Amanda lead an exemplary life; but alas, who can control their fate! at the end of that time she fell in with a young German, whose profession it was to tune piano fortes, and soon fell a victim to his seductive arts. The affair was at length discovered by the mother herself, who caught the parties one evening, in *flagrante delicto*[9] in an attic, but enough, the contemplation of their sin, is too dreadful to dwell upon. Mrs. Green certainly thought it too vile for toleration and Amanda and her paramour, were *vi et armis,*[10] turned out of doors.

No resource was left her but open prostitution, and she accordingly took to that degraded calling, has followed it two years and now remains in it, another unhappy victim sacrificed at the altar of man's brutal passions. May those who have not yet sinned, take warning by her example. In person, Amanda Green is tall, very tall; her form is full, her complexion clear, and altogether she is very handsome. She resides at Mrs. Shannon's, No. 74 West Broadway.

---

[8] *Negus* is a drink of wine and hot water, flavored with nutmeg, lemon, and sugar.

[9] To catch someone *in flagrante delicto* is to catch a person in the act of committing a crime.

[10] *Vi et armis* is Latin for by force and arms.

By dint of long and patient investigation, we have at length gathered all the necessary particulars in the course of a harlot who assumes the title of the Countess de Valcour, and shall very shortly give them to our readers. We intend to cut down these strumpet noblesse.[11] Next in order will follow Sophy Austin, Julia Brown, Mrs. Lewis, C—r's woman, &c. &c.

[11] *Strumpet noblesse* can be roughly defined and translated as noble whore.

24

WHIP

Excerpts

July 9, 1842

When George Wooldridge of the Whip *faced indictment for obscenity in 1842, these particular articles—"The Battery Spy," "The Libertine Dr. B," and "Pictures from Fancy No 2"—were named in the indictment papers. They are good examples of writing that was considered "racy" in 1842.*

The Battery Spy

On Thursday afternoon we visited this delightful spot, and during our promenade noticed the following ladies, whose bearing elicited the admiration of all roués, libertines[12] and sportsmen present, not neglecting the higher classes who wear goat-beards and moustache, and are self-styled gentlemen, but by us more rightly called suckers, sharps, diners-out, pimps, and drummers with white hats.

The elegant Mary Smith was there—dressed in the most splendid costume we ever saw—it was rich with simplicity, elegant with neatness.

[12] *Roués [and] libertines* are, in this context, persons without moral restraint.

Excerpts from *Whip* 2, no. 1 (July 9, 1842): 2.

Two splendid Belles from New Orleans, whom we have not the pleasure of knowing.

The superb Mary Capito, far more blooming than ever, dressed in the heighth of fashion.

The Misses Thompson and Clifton, and the lovely Misses Howes and Burke. The magnificent Mary Turner and Rose Berri both received much attention from the promenaders, who in an instant discovered them to be strangers, and many a wish was sighed for their quick return, as they glided from the battery.

Miss Emma Place made a splendid appearance on horseback; her costume we thought beautiful.

Harriet Grandy, dirty, slovenly and disgusting as usual.

The Libertine Dr. B

The upper crust soaplock,[13] Dr. B. is most respectfully informed that his actions towards a married lady in Walker street, has drawn upon him the eye of one who is determined to thwart his villainous designs; and to satisfy him of the truth of our remarks, we would ask him if he remembers the intellectual butcher. If not satisfied at this, we have some of your love letters in our possession, which were written to a married lady while you were absent from the city last winter. If you are wise, you will know how to regulate your conduct in future.

Pictures from Fancy No 2

Again FANCY calls upon us and we are her willing slave. Aeriel[14] floating on the perfumed air, points with her golden wand to her Tablet of Names and with witching smiles invites us to begin, and we obey.

Her form as perfect as the Venus of Conova[15]—her visage oval and of matchless beauty. Her dark hair fastened by a rare gem entwine her brow. Her language eloquent and voice sweet—her eye needs but rest on the object, it would captivate, and thus it ever should be, for Aeriel says 'tis *Miss Elizabeth Melville.*

---

[13]A *soaplock* is a rowdy. The term derives from the hairstyle sported by early nineteenth-century roughs, in particular the long locks at each side in front that were soaped to hold their shape.

[14]Probably Ariel, an angel important in British literature and a mischievous sprite in William Shakespeare's *The Tempest.*

[15]*Venus of Conova* is likely a reference to the statue by Antonio Canova, *Pauline Borghese as Venus,* 1808.

How are we to keep pace—for Fancy would now have *Miss Rose Berri* pictured. To do so we must fancy a fair one whose face denotes beauty and whose pleasing conversation would hold an anchorite a willing prisoner, she being of such graceful carriage and modest demeanor. But see, another leaf is turned and our eyes rest on the name of *Miss Mary C. Somers*—a sweet one, who as yet has scarce passed her sixteenth summer and whose merry laugh and boyant spirits tell that she is happy, not with a life of guilt but in possessing him she adores.

In our next we shall fancy

Ellen Thompson,
Emily Guilbert,
Mary Capito.

25

WHIP

Our Tenth Walk about Town; or, Nights in Gotham
December 24, 1842

In 1842, George Wooldridge of the Whip *was found guilty of publishing obscene material and sentenced to the "Tombs," the house of detention in New York City that took its name from the Egyptian details of its architecture. Immediately following his conviction, Wooldridge made a ritualistic promise to reform. The* Whip *did not change, however, and the weekly continued to publish "Walks about Town," containing news about prostitutes and brothels. In 1843, the courts were successful in bringing about the demise of the* Whip *and other sporting papers.*

...The next evening we were out with the last glimmer of day all rigged for our night among the fallen. We first rapped at the door of Celeste Thebault's. This was our visit, and we felt somewhat in doubt as to the manner of our reception. But her lively and buoyant self came to admit us, and from her manner we were assured she was right glad to see our *statue* enter in her snug, clean, and neatly furnished apartments. We found seated upon a sofa the pretty Maria, Eliza Green and Jane Thompson, Cad Oakley, who has still some shame, at least we thought so, by finding she had left the residence of old Miller in disgust. There was also Celeste['s] sister, a fine, portly looking lady, as was also the other ladies who were present. On our way we stopped at French Margarets, a keeper of one of our most private houses. Here we were favored with a view of that magnificent creature who resided with Mrs. Morgan in Reade street, and who we once described as the belle of the golden tassels. At Mrs. Sweets we were ushered into the front parlor on account of the McK's being in the back one—ever and anon we could hear their throats open and laugh at their own zests—pretty high boys these and deserve a place upon the pages of our Whip—full of fun, fond of frolick, and very often blamed for acts they are not guilty of. Maria we found as reserved as ever, while Jane Morris looked grum, but her spirits soon revived and she was herself again. Eveline looked well, as did the Driver—Adelaide full of business on account of the hostess being always on the go, showing anxious visitors the baby. Every one who was blest with a sight of it, freely calls for his bottle and drinks to his voyage to Italy. At the Duchesses we found her ladies enjoying themselves in the most elegant manner with some half dozen French gentleman who had the magnificent large centre table covered with champaigne and superb iced plum cake. As a stranger we were invited to partake, which after overcoming our *bashful* nature we consented, and as we raised the sparkling glass to our lips, we drank to the dark and splendid eye of the Melleville, the vivacity of Cappito, and the dignity of the Duchess, and while the Johnny crappoes responded to it with a three times three we saw another emptying gold in the lap of the elegant Melville, which reminded us much of the fall of Dianna.*[16] As we passed along we found a gentleman craving for admittance; she could not admit him because an officer was in the house searching for

---

*Is this the Goddes that fell by the fall of gold—COMPOSITOR.

[16] *The fall of Dianna* most likely is a reference to one of the many paintings dealing with the legend of Danaë. Zeus fell in love with Danaë, princess of Argos, and turned himself into a shower of gold, which fell on Danaë's lap, impregnating her with her son Perseus. In the nineteenth century, paintings of this mythological subject were sometimes seen as representations of prostitution, involving the exchange of money for sex.

a pocket book that was lost there. We passed on to the domicile of the Lyons, who we were pleased to find had returned from Boston after a chit chat about matters and things, and shake of the hand with Howes, Hastings, and a new Boston female, we took our departure south in quest of quiet and repose.

26

WHIP

Sodomites

January 29, 1842

Although it is rare to find any discussion in newspapers of homosexuality, the sporting papers did fume against those it called "Sodomites," perhaps because these men seemed to pose a particular threat to a male world that put a high value on heterosexual pleasures of the flesh.

THE SODOMITES.—We hope that in presenting to our readers a sketch of some of the inhuman enormities that a set of *fiends* bearing the form of men are nightly in the habit of disgusting nature with their monstrous and wicked acts; our excuse must be, that we have undertook to rout from our city these monsters. That it will be a Herculean task, we are well aware, yet we feel assured that in the end we shall be the conquerors.

We know them all by sight, and most of them by name. They are nearly all young men of rather genteel address, and of feminine appearance and manners; among this herd of beasts is one or two old and lecherous villains whom we know well, one of them already to our knowledge, has murdered, aye, that's the word, for by no calmer word can we call the brutal act, that caused a youth of our acquaintance, who was so unfortunate as to fall within the snare of this old sodomite and his beastly crew; he fell into a decline which so emaciated his form that when his body was raised from his bed to be placed within the grave, that the stiffness and coldness of the dead gave place to the shrunken and disjointed corpse.

To what has New York come, if this intolerable nuisance is continued much longer. Our city within the vicinity of the Park will become a second Palais Royale.[17] Their the agents of a horror stricken crime are men or rather miscreants, wearing the appearance of the human form also, their is no difference between the doings of these fiendish agents of the Palais Royale and the brutal sodomites of New York; their diabolical enticements lead to the same end. Fear seizes the mind of the moral man when he is thus accosted and his first instinct is to escape; who would appear at the police office even to prefer a charge against one of these abominable sinners, why no one in the world; yet we have the names of men who have been acted upon by these fiends, and when we want them, they will be called upon by a tribunal that they dare not refuse to obey—the Law.—

Men of respectability are frequently made the victims of extortion by them, for even death is preferable to the remotest connection with such a charge, we shall pursue this subject again, and endeavor to call the attention of Justices Matsell and Parker to it, for of a verity we are taught to think these horrible offenses foreign to our shores—to our nature they certainly are—yet they are growing a pace in New York—the why and the wherefore in the progress of our strictures we will endeavor to arrive at, as we know where these felons resort for the purpose of meeting and making appointments with their victims, who are generally young men of most prepossessing looks, yes we even know where these abominable and horrid stews are kept, in which these enormities are committed. To show these wretches that we are in earnest in what we say, we will merely ask, Collins Johnson and Adly if they do not believe us.

[17]A reference to the Palais-Royal in Paris, where commercial arcades became a place of assignation for male homosexuals in the nineteenth century.

27

FLASH

Our Indictments
December 11, 1841

Indicted, convicted, and later jailed for obscenity, the Flash *editor William Joseph Snelling (1804–1848) offered a clever, albeit tongue-in-cheek, defense of his language and subject matter.*

A lady once complimented Dr. Johnson[18] on the cleanliness of his famous dictionary. She was glad, she said, to find that there were no naughty words in it. —"I see, Madam," said the sturdy moralist, "that you have been looking for them."

On another occasion, when a lady was deploring that the sublime and beautiful book of Job[19] should be disfigured by indelicate imagery and dirty expressions—"Madam," said the Doctor; "the dirt is all in your own imagination."

We make no comments on the indictment found against three persons in this city, supposed to be editors and proprietors of the Flash, for a libel on the character of Mr. Myer Levy. It would be indecorous, to say the least, to bespeak the public opinion on a case that is to be tried by an impartial jury. It is not for us, but for twelve men, good and true, to decide whether the matter alluded to is a libel and, if it is, to say who is guilty of it; whether one, two or more, and that it then becomes the province of a court to apportion the punishments of the criminals, if such there be, to their respective degrees of guilt. Every man to his business; the jury to sift the alleged libel, the judge to pass sentence and we to publish the Flash; but upon the two other indictments against the same persons, we have a few remarks to make, without invading the rights and privileges of any oee [one].

The indictments charge, in substance, that the Flash is an immoral

---

[18]*Dr. Johnson* is Samuel Johnson, famous for his *Dictionary of the English Language* (1755).
[19]*The book of Job* is one of the books of the Bible from the Old Testament.

"Our Indictments," *Flash* 1, no. 16 (Dec. 11, 1841): 2.

and indecent paper, and calculated to incite improper and prurient feelings in the bosoms of the citizens. *Query*—what is immoral and indecent? We see a man lying, beastly drunk, in the street and a very indecent spectacle it is. We put him in a cart and convey him to the bar of the Police Court, thereby making his shame more manifest, and his punishment a more striking example. Is our proceeding, in this case, immoral or indecent? In like manner, we see an outcast from virtue and decency in the daily and nightly practice of vices infinitely more revolting and of more evil example than drunkenness, whom the laws, alas, for their imperfection! cannot reach, and we drag him or her to the bar of public opinion. Is our conduct immoral or indecent?

It seems, however, that the language we use is too coarse for the religiously refined nerves of Mr. Boggs[20] & the latter day saints;[21] men that would rather sit contentedly and inhale the odor of a dung-hill than command it to be removed by its proper name. These are the fellows who revel over the foul pages of the Herald[22] and McDowell's Journal[23] and put clouts upon the Chanting Cherubs. Such are those that pass through the Five Points without finding anything amiss and yet quarrel with the Sunday newsboys and vote the Adam and Eve of Dabufe[24] immoral and indecent. Gentlemen; most righteous, virtuous, and delicate gentlemen, the dirt of the Flash is all in your own imagi-nations. You have been looking for naughty words, and it is no wonder that you have found them. If your procreative sensibilities had not been morbidly acute, never would you have dreamed that those of oth-ers could be excited by anything that has yet appeared in the Flash. . . .

If to hold a villainy up to abhorance and execration; if to attack vice with the weapons of truth, sarcasm, ridicule and invective be immoral and indecent, then are the editors of the Flash indeed guilty—other-

---

[20] *Mr. Boggs* refers to William G. Boggs, one of the members of the Grand Jury that indicted Snelling and his coeditors of the *Sunday Flash.* Boggs had read to the court the jury's more general statement on the need for regulation of Sunday papers and was especially critical of their sale by newsboys. Boggs was the publisher of William Cullen Bryant's Democratic *Evening Post;* Snelling perceived him as an interested party to his case. Snelling also thought Boggs had been influenced by recent ministerial condemna-tion of the sporting press.

[21] *The latter day saints* is Snelling's way of putting down the religious allegiance of Boggs and the other jurors.

[22] Refers to the New York *Herald* founded by James Gordon Bennett in 1835, an early, inexpensive daily paper, as an example of what was called the penny press.

[23] A weekly newspaper created by John R. McDowall, containing information about prostitution in New York City.

[24] In mentioning the *Chanting Cherubs* and the *Adam and Eve of Dabufe,* Snelling was likely referring to local controversies that are at present unknown.

wise they have nothing to fear. We defy anyone to shew a single paragraph in our columns, a single sentence, a single line, that the utmost ingenuity of man can construe into an incentive to lewdness. On the other hand, we can point to hundreds of criminals whom we have hanged in chains by the highways as mute guides to others to the roads, from which they themselves have strayed.

One of the articles alleged to be imoral. . . . Two other items are the lives of Jane Dixon and Amanda Green; in which two of the most notorious and profligate strumpets in New York, or, indeed in the world, are flayed alive, and this merited castigation, forsooth, is immoral. . . .

Why do they begin with us? Let them punish the publishers of Dean Swift.[25] Let them suppress Byron. There is more seduction in Don Juan than a thousand Flashes. Let them present the Bible itself. It will puzzle them to find anything in our columns half so nasty as the command of the Lord to Ezekiel, or aught so revolting to delicacy as the crime of Onan, the incest of the patriarch, Judah, the rape of Tamar by her brother, Ammon, or the adultery of Bathsheba. The Bible speaks plainly, and calls things by their right names, and it is inspiration. We do the same, though with much less grossness, and it is obscenity. . . .

We deny that there has been anything profame immoral or indecent in the Flash from the time it came into being to the present day; unless it is all three to call a dog a son of a bitch. The charge is false *in toto*[26] and the indictments are mere humbugry, devised to prevent us from publishing our paper by holding us to heavy bail.

---

[25]*Dean Swift* is Jonathan Swift (1667–1745), Dean of St. Patrick's Cathedral 1714–1745, best known for his *Gulliver's Travels*.
[26]Totally.

28

P. F. HARRIS

Advertisement

February 19, 1855

In 1855, to promote his list of books, New York publisher Prescott F. Harris began publishing a weekly newspaper, the Broadway Belle. *On his advertised list were the racy books of American authors such as George Thompson, works of fiction regarded as erotic in their day, and texts that provided sexual information.*

Books That Are Books

To those who wish books that are in reality worth reading, we would be pleased to call their attention to the following list of original writings, from the pens of some of the most celebrated authors, not only in America, but Europe. Any of these works can be had at our office, or sent by mail to any part of the world, on receipt of the price in bills, silver, or postage satmps, in a letter (post-paid) directed to the Publisher of this paper, P. F. HARRIS, 102 Nassau street. N.Y.

Any five 25 cent books for one dollar; two 50 cent books and one 25 cent book for one dollar.

Evil Genius	25c
Sharps and Flats	25c
Julia King	25c
The Lame Devil	25c
The Irish Widow	25c
Harriet Wilson, by herself	25c
Paul the Profligate	25c
Adventures of a Country Girl	25c

P. F. Harris, bookseller, advertisement, *Broadway Belle,* Feb. 19, 1855.

29

GEORGE THOMPSON

From *The Mysteries of Bond Street*
1857

George Thompson (1823–ca. 1873), the most prolific American author of sensational fiction in the 1840s and 1850s, often wrote about persons of wealth, underworld figures, sexual acts of great variety, and contrasting neighborhoods of wealth and poverty in the city. In this story, John (Jack) Mickle, a young man on the town, goes with his friend Fred Bevans to a brothel in Five Points, a New York neighborhood that was home to many poor immigrants and free African Americans. There he encounters Mary Sanders, once his fiancée, who relates to him her story of seduction and subsequent life of prostitution. Her narrative takes her from the heights of New York's Bond Street to the depths of the slums of Five Points.

"Well, Mickle," said Fred, there is no more fun to-night, and as I don't feel like going to bed yet for an hour or so, suppose we take a cruise around the points, I've got the blues, and you don't appear to be in much better trim, and we may both fish up fun enough to cheer us up. I've got a few dollars left, we can take a dance at Pete Williams.[27] . . .

"I'll go it Fred, for I want something to chace away the double-breasted horrors,"[28] said Mickle taking his friend's arm, as they left the gambling house, and sauntered down Pell street. "I've not felt like myself all day." . . .

"Ah Mick, you have been letting your old Jersey sweetheart trouble you again, I am afraid. . . .

. . . Here is something to cheer us up—do you hear that fiddle squeak? . . .

The house which the two friends entered stood and stands to this

---

[27]Here Thompson mentions a real place. Pete Williams, an African American, had a famous dance hall in the Five Points area of New York.
[28]The term *double-breasted horrors* likely means a really severe fright.

George Thompson, *The Mysteries of Bond Street; or, The Seraglios of Upper Tendom* (New York: n.p., 1857).

day on the corner of Little Water and Anthony street. It was one of the worst of the vile dens that invested the horrible neighborhood at that period. There was scarcely a police officer from Maine to Georgia but what was acquainted in a professional way with the villainous proprietor who had made more than one journey to and from the States Prison. He was a tall, dark man, of a powerful frame; though the dissipated life that he had led for years, had evidently brought on the consumption, and when he was troubled with a fit of coughing, his tirade of blasphemies was so terrible that not even the miserable and degraded beings by whom he was surrounded, could repress a shudder. The bar was decorated with some half-dozen decanters, filled with drugged and poisonous liquors, interspersed with a few plaster of Paris images, the refuse lot of some wandering Italian. The girls who sheltered under the roof, were of course the lowest class of courtezans. . . . When Mickle and his friend entered the bar room, a blind negro was playing on a cracked fiddle, the tune of "money musk," and some of the inmates were performing, what is called a "straight four." . . .

. . . One of the girls who was dancing with a drunken sailor gave a wild shriek, and fainted away. . . .

Mickle and Fred lifted up the fainting girl, and held a glass of water to her lips, which restorative brought her somewhat to her senses. She gazed wildly round the room, until at last her eyes appeared to be riveted upon the features of Mickle, and she at length exclaimed, in choking tones: "Dear John, don't you—don't you know me?"

"No! I never saw you before, to my knowledge, in the whole course of my life," said Mickle, with amazement, while he scanned every feature of her bloated countenance. Who, in the name of heaven, are you!"

"Gallus Kate,[29] of the Five Points, once the pure and virtuous Mary Sanders, of Morristown, New Jersey!" was the startling reply. . . .

The Courtezan's Story

. . . Pen cannot describe the anguish that rended the heart of John Mickle, when he discovered in gallus Kate of the Five Points, the girl to whom he had given his fondest affections, the once beautiful Mary Sanders. Though what is commonly called in the parlance of the term,

---

[29] *Gallus Kate* is a nickname that used one of the common tricks of slang, turning bad to good. The term *gallus* was probably derived from gallows and tended to mean originally down and out; by the 1840s it was used playfully to mean exciting, cocky, rakish, or tough.

a fast young man about town . . . he still had a heart to pity and commiserate her unhappy condition. Being possessed of some little means apart from his trade, he consulted with his friend, Fred Bevans, who gave his advice in the matter, and finally came to the conclusion to act the part of a philanthrophist by hiring apartments for her, where she could maintain herself by honest labor, until he could devise some future plan for her welfare.

Mary gladly acquiesced to his proposition, for she had never been a willing votary to the fearful calling in which unfortunate circumstances had placed her. Like the repentant Magdalen, she wished to tread again the path of virtue; but hitherto, wherever she had made an appeal to her own sex, they had scoffed at the idea of her ever being considered beyond the rank of Leper or Pariah. . . .

Her old lover and benefactor has called upon her to-day, to learn from her own lips the tale of her wrongs. . . .

"You remember, John, the large and beautiful green that stands in front of Luce's tavern, in our own dear native village, where we used often to walk of a moonlight evening, ere you left to try your fortunes in this great city? Well, there it was I first met the betrayer of my virtue. Though a good looking man, with the instinctive feeling that guards a virtuous bosom, I thought I could perceive something of evil in his ardent gaze, when I first met him; blushing scarlet, I dropped my veil and resolved to shun his path in future. . . . About this time your letters ceased to come to me, and though it wrung my heart to think so, I surmised that in the society of some city belle, you had forgotten your village sweetheart, Mary Sanders. A person advised Hurdell of this matter, and he shortly afterwards solicited an introduction, and I, wearied with his importunity, at last granted it. He pressed his suit immediately with the most ardent professions of love, but I gave him no encouragement, and finally told him that my heart was irrevocably anothers. He appeared much chagrined at my firm declaration, but plead that we might often meet in future, at least as friends. His request was reasonable, and I complied. . . .

"One day while engaged in pleasant converse, Hurdell asked me if ever I had heard of the new sciences of Psychology and animal magnetism, that were just then exciting so much astonishment in scientific circles. I told him I had read something concerning them in a few of the journals of the day, but so little as not to understand the theory of them."[30]

---

[30]Thompson plays on the fear in his era that learned men, such as the dentist Hurdell, might use hypnotism to seduce women.

"Ah! then, you have missed enjoying some of the most pleasing sensations you can imagine, however, if you are willing to be my pupil it will take but a short period to make you an adept, for I am a thorough professor of these most wonderful sciences."

"My curiosity was aroused, and acceded to his proposal, promising myself an infinite fund of amusement with my companions when I became a finished scholar.

"Hurdell professed to admire my resolution and promised if I would call at his rooms, at the hotel, on the following day, he would give me my first lesson, to initiate me in the mysteries of these strange sciences.

"I did not fail to keep the appointment, and Hurdell's smile, with a cordial greeting received me. . . .

"I took a seat upon the sofa, as Hurdell suggested, and he instantly commenced passing his hands over my forehead with a gentle, scarce perciptible touch of feeling, while his dark eyes were fixed with an intense, snake like fascination on mine. The sensations he aroused, soon became of the most pleasing description. I felt as if the cares of the world were forgotten. A sort of balmy sleep stole upon me, my spirits were buoyant and light as air for a short space of time followed by a period of misty darkness, and then, John Mickle, your affianced bride was in the power of an unprincipled magnetizer. The victim was in his power, incapable of resistance, and he, villain, as he was, prepared to take advantage of a helpless maiden, but although I was in a perfectly helpless state when he attempted to consummate the unholy sacrifice, a convulsive shudder shook my frame.

"The base scoundrel wished to tarnish a willing victim, and noticing my tremor, gave me the last terrible proof of his power, he whispered in my ear: 'Nay, dearest, do not tremble. You know dear Mary, that I am John Mickle, your lawful husband. I have returned from the city and made you my lawful wife, and you must not dearest, receive my advances coldly on the bridal night.' . . .

"My brutal ravisher seeming to me the dearest of husbands, took all the liberties of a husband, and I deeming him such, had no inclination to resist his advances. Those famous sciences which placed in the hands of honorable men, serve to astonish the world, had been used by a demon to work my destruction. I can say truly, that I sinned in innocence, but partly awoke from the terrible and miraculous dream of langour.

"Like the harmless dove in the terrible coils of the rattle-snake, I saw in a mirror that I was in the lascivious embrace of doctor Hurdell, and not in a fond husband's arms. I struggled to free myself, though but faintly, for his cold gleaming eyes were instantly fastened on mine, raising a spell as powerful to my imagination, as the miracles of holy writ, for as true as heaven, I deemed what he asserted true.

"I was past resistance. My betrayer triumphed, and when I awoke from my trance, I felt, while the blush of shame crimsoned my cheek, that I was a dishonored girl. . . .

"For a week after we came to the city," she continued, "Hurdell was very kind and attentive. He strove by every means in his power to banish from my mind ideas and recollections of former virtue. I soon found out that the house in which he had established me as his mistress was of that peculiar class that landlords let at enormous rents to noted procuresses for the purpose of illicit pleasure. There were three other tenants, all beautiful young girls—one at least not over sixteen, who was the mistress of a wealthy Wall street broker—and the other two, who were somewhat older, the paramours of two down town merchants, who passed for respectable members of society.

"It appeared to be an arranged plan with these voluptuaries, who were linked together by an oath of mutual secrecy, to render their victims as callous to every moral feeling as possible.

"At first I felt shocked at the obscene jests and ribaldry of my elder sisters in sin, but the feelings soon wore off, and wearied with enui, the bane of the harlots' life, I grew familiar with their manners, and was glad to associate with my trail companions. . . .

"Day by day my mind became more and more corrupt. I no longer shuddered at the ribald jests of my companions, and a blush no longer mantled my check, at the most open language. . . .

"There was a library for the benefit of the house, and in the first few days of my initiation I endeavored in vain among its voluminous contents, to find a fac simile of the dear old family Bible, that always lay upon the table at my fond mother's cottage, in the country. Alas! what consolation could I find in the libidinous experience of The Lustful Turk, Betty Ireland, Fanny Hill, or The Two Cousins; and yet in the first stages of harlotry there is a strange desire to peruse these detestable volumes; a desire that turns gradually to a deadly hatred, when the victim becomes the prey of all men possessed of a sufficient stipend to purchase her favor.[31] . . .

"I had received overtures on several occasions from a rich railroad

---

[31]Thompson is linking the erotic books of his day (with which he was closely associated) to Mary Sanders's downfall.

contractor, who dwelt in a palace in Bond street; but up to this period I had always repelled them with indignation and scorn. Hurdell's infidelity steeled my heart to the last remaining sense of virtue; my whole being was a wreck, doomed from that hour to drift on the ocean of despair, and I threw myself into the arms of a man at least sixty years of age.

"This eccentric individual, who was as ugly in person as he was recreate in mind, had, by means of his immense wealth, gathered around him six of the most beautiful women in America.

"And I, in a moment of mad frenzy, had agreed to be the companion of these creatures, who sold themselves for gold. Virtue and the lowliest station of life should have been preferable to this existence of deathless shame.

"If I had reason to complain of the miserly meanness of my former protector, I had a surfeit of every luxury in my new home. The costliest viands were purchased from the most eminent caterers to cheat the palate. The most luscious wines were always upon his tables, (and in which I soon learned to drown recollection and remorse) and this Sybarite of the nineteenth century, who emulated the Mormons of the Desert,[32] in the heart of the Empire City, who had not one redeeming trait in his character, if I except the criminal profusion of squandering what would have made hundreds of poor families happy, held a high position in society, on account of his wealth; and many an intriguing mother of the Fifth Avenue would have been ravished with the idea, if he had proffered his heart and hand in marriage to her no less intriguing daughter. . . .

"You may be sure, dear John, that, detesting him as I did, I could not long be the recipient of his bounty, and I left him to become the mistress of a young and handsome man, who swore eternal fidelity and love. His name was Arnold Lee, and though his fortune was far inferior to my former protector, I felt that with him I should find peace, if not happiness.

"I soon found that his oaths and protestations of love were a base lie. . . .

. . . [I] became the paramour of a gambler, one of those birds of prey that feed on society. . . . It was a continual warfare between luxury and want, for a period of twenty months—and then I became what you found me, in the vile den on the Five Points."

---

[32]Thompson is making an association between male promiscuity and Mormon polygamy that was common in his day.

30

DR. J. HENRY

Henry's Private Adviser

1856

In the 1850s, entrepreneurs attempted to make money by offering to sell new techniques of contraception. In Henry's Private Adviser, *for example, Dr. J. Henry of Rossville, Maryland, sought to sell his "Chart of Life," a guide to what today is called the rhythm method of contraception, drawing without acknowledgment on Frederick Hollick's* The Marriage Guide.

Vol. 1, No. 1
Oct. 15. 1856

THE GREAT DISCOVERY OF THE NINETEENTH CENTURY!
40,000 Copies sold in one Month!!

THE CHART OF LIFE;
OR,
THEORY OF RE-PRODUCTION,
*and Rules of the Prevention of Offspring, without Medicine
and without Mechanical Contrivances, and without
Restriction of Sexual Intercourse only at
Short stated periods.*

IN FACT,
THE GREATEST BOON
THAT HAS BEEN VOUCHSAFED TO SUFFERING HUMANITY
IN THIS FRUITFUL AGE OF GREAT DISCOVERIES.

BY J. HENRY, M.D.

When the Divine Being created man, He commanded him to "Be fruitful and multiply, and replenish the earth." And, however often His

---

Dr. J. Henry, *Henry's Private Adviser*, 1856.

other commands may have been violated, there is no disputing the fact, that this first command has been, and still is, well and faithfully kept. When man was first created in perfect health, with the whole world before him for his domain, there could have been no reason why this command should not have been strictly fulfilled. But in a later day, when the seeds of disease and death have fastened upon a large portion of the human race—when the earth has become crowded with inhabitants, it is well to investigate this command, before we too blindly follow it. And in so doing we shall find many, very many, instances wherein it had better be disregarded. . . .

To this enjoyment there is but one serious drawback, viz.: the consequences which follow, either in bringing into existence large families, or the dangers and perils often attending child-birth.

Many persons are so circumstanced as to render it extremely inconvenient to support a large family. With two or three children they could move along in life comfortably, but when that number is increased to eight or ten, then indeed, the burden becomes oppressive, ruining the mother's health, and hastening her to an untimely grave; and grinding down the father with a crushing force, keeping him struggling through life for a bare subsistence, and utterly forbidding him ever to rise from beneath the gripping hand of poverty.

Again, one or both of the parents may be consumptive, or scrofulous,[33] or afflicted with some other hereditary disease; thus entailing these frightful maladies upon a harmless, inoffensive and innocent offspring. . . .

To obviate these difficulties, and still allow the gratification of the animal propensities, or, in other words, to devise some plan by which sexual intercourse could be allowed without producing conception or child-birth, has been the study of medical men for many years, but until lately without success. The French, who have ever devoted the most time and labor in investigating this subject, at first introduced a covering for the male organ, which was used during the sexual act. But this is not only inconvenient but very annoying and irritating to the female, often producing violent inflammation. A host of preventive powders next followed, and were extensively advertised, but these do not act as a preventive to conception, but kill and expel the child after its formation has commenced; and this violent expulsion always injures the mother more or less, and often fatally.

---

[33] *Scrofulous* meant that one was suffering from a form of tuberculosis characterized mainly by enlargement of the lymph nodes.

But science gradually unfolded the theory and mode of conception, until it remained for the celebrated and indefatigable Dr. M. Negrier, of Paris, after a severe and protracted investigation of the matter, to completely unfold the theory and manner of conception; and to discover a mode by which sexual congress could be freely allowed without the least danger of pregnancy arising therefrom. In fact, if his directions are obeyed, conception is utterly impossible. And what renders the discovery all the more valuable, is the fact that NO MEDICINE of any kind, either externally or internally, is required. No precautions or instrumentalities of any kind are taken, but all rests upon the particular period in which the act takes place. The substance of the discovery is this. *At certain distinct periods, if the sexual act is performed, conception will invariably follow, if the organs are in perfect health. At no other time can it take place, under any circumstances whatsoever....*

But it remained for Dr. J. Henry to methodize these discoveries— divest them of all technical and reduce them to simply concise rules, capable of being practically understood by the large mass of the community.... Dr. Henry has prepared a work entitled the CHART OF LIFE, embodying the cream of the discoveries of Negrier and others, together with the result of his own observations. This work is divested of all technicalities and superfluities calculated to hinder rather than enlighten the understanding of the masses.

The sale of the work at once became immense, and still continues so, and a host of testimonials are flowing in upon him from all directions. As many persons feel a delicacy about inquiring at a book-store for a work of this kind, Dr. H. determined to forward it *only* by *mail*. This plan has been strictly adhered to, and has given satisfaction to all parties, and will be still continued. No bookseller or traveling agent will have it for sale, but it will be sent invariably through the mail, thoroughly enveloped and closely sealed, so as to be impervious to the eyes of prying postmasters' clerks; and all communications and orders will be held strictly confidential. The price of this "Chart," in consequence of its unprecedented sale, has been reduced to ONE DOLLAR per copy, on receipt of which it will be forwarded, *post paid, by letter postage,* which makes it a *penitentiary offence for any one to open it, except the person to whom it is directed.* It will also be closely sealed. Bills on any solvent bank are received, and all money sent at his risk, provided a note of the amount is left with the postmaster when mailed.

Below are selected a few of the many testimonials which have been received; only suppressing names as all communications are considered strictly confidential: —

SYRACUSE, N.Y., Dec. 15, 1855

DR. HENRY:

DEAR SIR, — Five years ago last fall I married my wife. She was then strong, robust and hearty. Eleven months after our marriage she was brought to childbed, and with much difficulty the child was taken from her by instruments. The physician then informed me that she would never give birth to a full grown child, and probably might die in the attempt. Twice since then I have been obliged to call the medical aid to procure abortion before the child was fully formed; but these efforts nearly ruined the health of my wife. About a year since I saw your circular, and immediately ordered your *Chart of Life*. I was at once struck with its exceeding beauty and simplicity, and instantly commenced obeying its rules. My wife's health rapidly improved, and we have not had, and I am confident never shall have again, occasion to procure another painful abortion. I would not take thousands of dollars and be deprived of the information it gives. May God bless you, and make you like the good Samaritan, a minister of mercy to many more suffering families.

Truly yours, A——C——.

NEWARK, N.J. Nov. 27, 1855

DR. HENRY:

DEAR SIR. — Your circular came into my hands about fifteen months since. I had long been contemplating the marriage state, but being young and in indigent circumstances, the prospect of a large family had deterred me. I ordered your *"Chart of Life,"* and upon reading it became at once satisfied of the truth of its theory. I immediately contracted marriage and following the rules have fully satisfied myself of their soundness and truth. As yet I have no sign of a family, but my circumstances have so much improved of late, that I really begin to think a lisping little cherub would be quite an addition to our happiness. Should we conclude to act upon this thought, we intend so to time it that the birth shall take place in the spring or fall, as we consider that a better season than in the cold of winter or burning heat of summer. Accept a thousand thanks for your valuable Chart. It has saved me its cost a thousand fold.

Ever yours, B —— E——.

31

JULIA GAYLOVE

Inez de Castro

May 23, 1857

In 1857, George Ackerman (d. 1873) ran a complex business. Under the name James Ramerio he published and sold sensational novels, Aristotle's Master-piece, racy fiction, and the weekly Venus' Miscellany. *The weekly often featured stories of high romantic fiction, in which European aristocrats and their ladies found their way to wed and bed. In contrast to accounts in the 1840s sporting papers, the fiction published by George Ackerman in the late 1850s portrayed sexual passion in explicit detail.*

[Inez de Castro, sold to a lowly miller as a wife, finds herself instead married to the governor of the town of Santiago, Don Manuel De Calvedos.]

"Inez," burst from the lips of Don Manuel.

"Oh, heavens! It is he—save me, save me," she cried, as rushing into his outstretched arms, her lovely form palpitating with a thousand emotions, the fair, soft ringlets swept his cheek for a moment, and the next she lay lifeless in his tender embrace. Who can picture the feelings of pride and love with which the fond lover gazed upon that pale face, as he bore her "gently as a ministering angel" to the couch in the adjoining room, and laying her upon it, set about restoring her to consciousness. It is needless to say how this was accomplished and how many tender words passed between the re-united lovers, suffice it to say, they soon forgot all but love, every other feeling but that of passion was o'ermastered, and the quick, warm kisses came quick and ardently, as the two sank gradually in happy forgetfulness upon the pillows, until the breath of each so co-mingled as to carry a soft electric thrill, and a flow of love from heart to heart, that sent the pulses thrilling, and the warm blood coursing madly through the veins of

Julia Gaylove, "Inez de Castro; or, the Intrigues of the Court of Isabel of Aragon," *Venus' Miscellany*, chap. 6, vol. 2, no. 2 (May 23, 1857): 2.

those two forms so moved by amorous emotions. Rapidly, but with a trembling hand, Don Manuel sought to raise the resisting drapery, that enviously clung around the most hidden beauties of her matchless form, and as each charm revealed itself to his desired touch, he pressed his lips involuntarily upon the blushing lillies [sic], that nestled at his breast. And then a soft white hand stole gently from around his neck, to press with fond and lingering delight, where its lightest touch had caused a thrill of rapture, almost to[o] intense to bear. His breast heaves, his breath comes quick and short, he almost writhes under the electric pressure of those taper fingers, yet they are not withdrawn in pity. But ah! the waxen limbs are powerless now, so excessive is the exstacy [sic] of bliss which fills her soul, as in retaliation, her lover bathes her in the essence of loves [sic] flower. Madly they sport in paradise a few short seconds. How gladly would he drink of the nectar of her rosy lips with his last breath, as his yielding form sinks alike with hers, powerless upon the couch.

32

JEAN ROSSEAU

Advertisements

January 31, 1857

Publisher George Ackerman used the business name "Jean Rosseau" for marketing his explicitly erotic publications, French imports, and condoms, advertised "To the Sporting Fraternity."

To the Sporting Fraternity,
JEAN ROSSEAU, IMPORTER OF
Transparent Cards, Cundums, etc., etc. Also, on hand the most complete assortment of all the modern patterns of Advantage Cards, which I will forward by mail, postage paid, at the following rates:

Jean Rosseau, Advertisements, *Venus' Miscellany* 1, no. 12 (Jan. 31, 1857): 3

Transparent cards per pack, ... $2 00
Advantage   do 1 50
Cundums for the prevention of conception, p'r doz. 2 00

N.B.—A liberal discount made to the trade.
All orders address,

JEAN ROSSEAU,
167 William-st., N.Y.

3

Coda: The Comstock Law of 1873

33

U.S. CONGRESS

An Act for the Suppression of Trade in, and Circulation of, Obscene Literature and Articles of Immoral Use

March 3, 1873

The New York Y.M.C.A. sent Anthony Comstock (1844–1915), a clerk and an anti-vice crusader, to lobby in Washington, D.C., for a strengthened federal anti-obscenity law. On March 3, 1873, Congress passed "An Act for the Suppression of Trade in, and Circulation of, Obscene Literature and Articles of Immoral Use," which became known as the Comstock Law. This federal statute made it illegal and punishable by fines or imprisonment or both to send through the mail six kinds of material: erotica; contraceptive medications or devices; abortifacients; sexual implements, such as those used in masturbation; contraceptive information; and advertisements for contraception, abortion, or sexual implements. State, or Little Comstock, laws soon followed, forbidding the sale of these items. Courts interpreted the Comstock laws to put under the ban books and pamphlets supporting free love or offering sex education, even when written in a scientific manner.

Chap. CCLVIII, "An Act for the Suppression of Trade in, and Circulation of, Obscene Literature and Articles of Immoral Use," *Congressional Globe,* 42nd Cong., 3rd sess., Appendix, p. 297.

Be it enacted by the Senate and House of Representatives of the United States of America in Congress ssembled [sic], That whoever, within that whoever [sic], within the District of Columbia, or either of the Territories, or other place within the exclusive jurisdiction of the United States, shall sell, or offer to sell, or shall give away, or offer to give away, or shall have in his or her possession with intent to sell or give away, any obscene or indecent book, pamphlet, paper, advertisement, drawing, lithograph, engraving, wood-cut, daguerreotype, photograph, stereoscopic picture, model, cast, instrument, or other article for indecent or immoral nature, or any article or medicine for the prevention of conception, or for causing abortion except on a prescription of a physician in good standing given in good faith, or shall advertise the same for sale, or shall write or print, or cause to be written or printed, any card, circular, book, pamphlet, advertisement, or notice of any kind, stating when, where, how, or of whom, or by what means, any of the said obscene or indecent articles, or those hereinbefore mentioned, can be purchased or obtained, or shall manufacture, draw, or expose to have sold or exposed, or shall print any such article, shall, on conviction thereof, be imprisoned at hard labor for not less than six months nor more than five years for each offense, or fined not less than $100, nor more than $2,000, with costs of court.

Sec. 2. That section one hundred and forty-eight of the act to revise, consolidate, and amend the statutes relating to the Post Office Department, approved June 8, 1872, be amended to read as follows:

"Sec. 148. That no obscene, lewd, or lascivious book, pamphlet, picture, paper, print, or other publication of an indecent character, or any article or thing designed or intended for the prevention of conception or procuring of abortion, nor any article or thing intended or adapted for any indecent or immoral use or nature, nor any written or printed card, circular, book, pamphlet, advertisement, or notice of any kind giving information, directly or indirectly, where, or how, or of whom, or by what means either of the things before mentioned may be obtained or made, nor any letter upon the envelope of which, or postal card upon which indecent or scurrilous epithets may be written or printed, shall be carried in the mail; and any person who shall knowingly deposit, or cause to be deposited, for mailing or delivery, any of the hereinbefore mentioned articles or things, or any notice or paper containing any advertisement relating to the aforesaid articles or things, and any person who, in pursuance of any plan or scheme for disposing of any of the hereinbefore mentioned articles or things, shall take or cause to be taken from the mail any such letter or package, shall be deemed guilty of a misdemeanor, and, on conviction thereof, shall, for every offense, be fined not less that $100 nor more that $5,000, or imprisoned at hard labor not less than one year nor more than ten years, or both, in the discretion of the judge."

Sec. 3. That all persons are prohibited from importing into the United States, from any foreign country, any of the hereinbefore-mentioned articles or things, except the drugs hereinbefore mentioned when imported in bulk, and not put up for any of the purposes before mentioned, under a penalty of $1,000 for each importation, to be imposed upon due conviction of such offense; and all such prohibited articles in the course of importation shall be seized by the officer of customs and condemned and destroyed.

Sec. 4. That whoever, being an officer, agent, or employee of the Government of the United States, shall knowingly aid or abet any person engaged in any violation of this act, shall be deemed guilty of a misdemeanor, and, on conviction thereof, shall, for every offense, be punished as provided in section two of this act.

Sec. 5. That any judge of any district or circuit court of the United States before whom complaint of any violation of this act shall be made, supported by oath or affirmation founded on knowledge or belief, may issue, comformably to the Constitution, a warrant directed to the marshal, or any deputy marshal, in the proper district, directing him to search for, seize, and take possession of any such obscene or indecent books, papers, articles, or things, and to make due and immediate return thereof, to the end that the same may be condemned and destroyed by proceedings, which shall be conducted in the same manner as other proceedings in case of municipal seizure.

A Chronology of the Literature of Sexual Conversation in Antebellum America (1684–1873)

1684   *Aristotle's Master-piece* first published in English, appearing in Boston within a year.

1765–
1769   William Blackstone issues *Commentaries on the Laws of England.*

1776   The Continental Congress adopts Declaration of Independence.

1789   George Washington becomes first president of the United States.

1790s   Advent of the Second Great Awakening, a revival movement that would reach a crescendo in the 1820s and 1830s.

1812   Lyman Beecher gives his sermon "A Reformation of Morals Practicable and Indispensable."

1825   Frances Wright comes to the United States to found Nashoba, a utopian experiment outside of Memphis, Tennessee.

1827   Lyman Beecher gives his sermon "Resources of the Adversary and Means of Their Destruction."

1829   Andrew Jackson becomes president.

1829   Charles Grandison Finney arrives in New York City to spearhead the Second Great Awakening revival movement in its later phase.

1829   Frances Wright opens the Hall of Science in New York City and begins publishing the *Free Enquirer* with Robert Dale Owen.

1830   Lyman Beecher delivers his sermon "The Perils of Atheism to the Nation."

1831   Robert Dale Owen publishes *Moral Physiology; or, a Brief and Plain Treatise on the Population Question.*

1831   John R. McDowall issues *The Magdalen Report: First Annual Report of the Executive Committee of the New-York Magdalen Society.*

1832   Charles Knowlton publishes *Fruits of Philosophy; or, the Private Companion of Young Married People.*

1832   Orson Squire Fowler converts to phrenology after listening to the lectures of Johann Spurzheim.

1832   Sylvester Graham achieves renown with lectures on the cholera epidemic.

1833   Benjamin Day begins publishing New York's first penny newspaper, the *Sun.*

1834   Sylvester Graham publishes *A Lecture to Young Men.*

1837   United States in throes of financial panic.

1838   Ann Trow Lohman begins to advertise her abortion services as Madame Restell.

1839   Mary S. Gove publishes *Solitary Vice: An Address to Parents and Those Who Have the Care of Children.*

1840   Luther V. Bell publishes *An Hour's Conference with Fathers and Sons, in Relation to a Common and Fatal Indulgence of Youth.*

1841   Weekly "flash" papers with names such as *Sunday Flash,* the *Whip,* and the *Rake* appear in New York City.

1841   Editors of the *Sunday Flash* are indicted for obscene libel, followed by the indictments of editors of several sporting papers in 1842.

1842   Congress prohibits the importation of all "indecent and obscene prints, paintings, lithographs, engravings, and transparencies" in Section 28 of the Tariff Act.

1842   Charles Knowlton publishes "Gonorrhoea Dormientium" in the *Boston Medical and Surgical Journal.*

1842   Lorenzo N. Fowler publishes *The Principles of Phrenology and Physiology Applied to Man's Social Relations; Together with an Analysis of the Domestic Feelings.*

1845   Frederick Hollick publishes *The Origin of Life: A Popular Treatise on the Philosophy and Physiology of Reproduction.*

1845   George Wilkes founds the *National Police Gazette.*

1846   Lorenzo N. Fowler publishes the 22nd edition of *Marriage: Its History and Ceremonies; with a Phrenological and Physiological Exposition of the Functions and Qualifications for Happy Marriages.*

1848   Mary S. Gove marries Thomas Low Nichols.

1848   The first women's rights convention takes place in Seneca Falls, New York.

1849   California Gold Rush begins.

1850 Frederick Hollick first publishes *The Marriage Guide.*

1851 Orson S. Fowler publishes *Love and Parentage, Applied to the Improvement of Offspring.*

1854 Thomas Low Nichols, with Mary S. Gove as likely coauthor of some sections, publishes *Esoteric Anthropology.*

1854 Thomas Low Nichols and Mary S. Gove Nichols publish *Marriage: Its History, Character, and Results.*

1855 Prescott F. Harris publishes *Broadway Belle* in New York, with advertisements for sensationalist novels by George Thompson and erotica.

1856 William Andrus Alcott publishes *The Physiology of Marriage.*

1857 George Ackerman publishes *Venus' Miscellany.*

1857 George Thompson publishes *The Mysteries of Bond Street; or, the Seraglios of Upper Tendom.*

1861– 1865 Civil War divides the nation.

1873 Congress passes the federal law for the "Suppression of Trade in, and Circulation of, Obscene Literature and Articles of Immoral Use," informally known as the Comstock Law.

Questions for Consideration

1. How did the authors of *Aristotle's Master-piece* and evangelical Christians differ in the way in which they understood sexual matters?
2. What new perspectives did moral physiologists bring to the public conversation about sex?
3. What were the critical differences between the ideas of freethinkers and Christian moral physiologists in their consideration of the body and sexual functioning?
4. What constituted sexual desire in *Aristotle's Master-piece*? In the writings of moral physiologists? What was desire's perceived relation to the body? To health and disease? Why was blood so important in early nineteenth-century understandings of sex? What part did the nerves play?
5. What did the different authors—for example, the writers of *Aristotle's Master-piece,* Lyman Beecher, Charles Knowlton, Mary Gove, and Thomas Low Nichols—consider to be the purposes of sexual intercourse?
6. Did those coming from different frameworks agree or disagree on whether sexual desire was a force for good or evil? Did writers on sex in antebellum America separate desire from love? Did they believe that the human goal was to satisfy sexual desire or to bring it under control? How did they perceive the relation of sexual expression to marriage?
7. What did Sylvester Graham and his followers see as the harms of masturbation? What were its symptoms? What were some of the methods to "cure" individuals of it? Why did the practice assume such importance in antebellum American sexuality?
8. Why was popular culture of the day, such as theater and novels, seen as dangerous by a writer such as Luther V. Bell?
9. Did phrenologists and others in the 1850s perceive men and women to be the same in regard to sexual relations and sexual pleasure? Did they perceive them to be different? If the latter, were the differences

inherent in their bodily structures or did they spring from their relations to each other and to children?

10. What did antebellum writers, such as Robert Dale Owen, Lorenzo Niles Fowler, Orson Squire Fowler, and Frederick Hollick, mean by "natural" when referring to sex and the body? By implication, what was "unnatural"? Why was discussion of the natural important to certain writers?

11. How did sexual enthusiasts such as Mary Gove and Thomas Low Nichols see the role of pleasure in sexual relations? Did it differ for men and women?

12. Which authors believed that men and women had the right to control their fertility? What were the methods available? How did opponents of contraception judge the harm it caused to the individual and the society? What did supporters of contraception see as the benefits?

13. According to the 1850s advertisements, what kinds of material did some booksellers offer?

14. What were some of the themes in 1850s "racy" and sensational fiction? Who was the projected audience? Why might this material have been entertaining to these imagined readers?

15. How did those opposed to the sale of erotic materials, such as the drafters of the Comstock Law, perceive the role of the state? What framework(s) for understanding sexuality guided them?

16. How do you think nineteenth-century readers were influenced by these various kinds of reading material? How might readers' beliefs and practices have been shaped by what they read? How did the existence of contending frameworks for understanding sexuality offer readers the ability to accept or reject what they read?

Selected Bibliography

GENERAL WORKS

Halttunen, Karen. *Confidence Men and Painted Women: A Study of Middle-Class Culture in America, 1830–1870*. New Haven, Conn.: Yale University Press, 1982.

Horowitz, Helen Lefkowitz. *Rereading Sex: Battles over Sexual Knowledge and Suppression in Nineteenth-Century America*. New York: Alfred A. Knopf, 2002; Vintage, 2003.

May, Henry F. *The Enlightenment in America*. New York: Oxford University Press, 1976.

Reynolds, David S. *Beneath the American Renaissance: The Subversive Imagination in the Age of Emerson and Melville*. New York: Alfred A. Knopf, 1988.

Thomas, Keith. *Man and the Natural World: A History of the Modern Sensibility*. New York: Pantheon Books, 1983.

CLASS, CULTURE, AND SEXUALITY IN THE CITY

Blumin, Stuart M. *The Emergence of the Middle Class: Social Experience in the American City, 1760–1900*. Cambridge, U.K.: Cambridge University Press, 1989.

Buckley, Peter. "To the Opera House: Culture and Society in New York City, 1820–1860." Ph.D. diss., State University of New York at Stony Brook, 1984.

Cockrell, Dale. *Demons of Disorder: Early Blackface Minstrels and Their World*. Cambridge, U.K.: Cambridge University Press, 1997.

Cohen, Patricia Cline. "The Helen Jewett Murder: Violence, Gender, and Sexual Licentiousness in Antebellum America." *NWSA Journal* 2 (1990): 374–80.

———. *The Murder of Helen Jewett: The Life and Death of a Prostitute in Nineteenth-Century New York*. New York: Alfred A. Knopf, 1998.

———. "Unregulated Youth: Masculinity and Murder in the 1830s City." *Radical History Review* 52 (1992): 33–52.

Dudden, Faye E. *Women in American Theater: Actresses and Audiences, 1790–1870.* New Haven, Conn.: Yale University Press, 1982.

Gilfoyle, Timothy J. *City of Eros: New York City, Prostitution, and the Commercialization of Sex, 1790–1920.* New York: W. W. Norton & Company, 1992.

Howell, Philip. "Sex and the City of Bachelors: Sporting Guidebooks and Urban Knowledge in Nineteenth-Century Britain and America." *Ecumene: A Journal of Environment, Culture, Meaning* 8 (Jan. 2001): 20–50.

Srebnick, Amy Gilman. *The Mysterious Death of Mary Rogers: Sex and Culture in Nineteenth-Century New York.* New York: Oxford University Press, 1995.

Stansell, Christine. *City of Women: Sex and Class in New York, 1789–1860.* New York: Alfred A. Knopf, 1986.

Stott, Richard B. *Workers in the Metropolis: Class, Ethnicity, and Youth in Antebellum New York City.* Ithaca, N.Y.: Cornell University Press, 1990.

Wilentz, Sean. *Chants Democratic: New York City and the Rise of the American Working Class, 1788–1850.* New York: Oxford University Press, 1984.

CONTRACEPTION AND ABORTION

Brodie, Janet Farrell. *Contraception and Abortion in Nineteenth-Century America.* Ithaca, N.Y.: Cornell University Press, 1994.

Browder, Clifford. *The Wickedest Woman in New York: Madame Restell, the Abortionist.* Hamden, Conn.: Archon Books, 1988.

Dayton, Cornelia Hughes. "Taking the Trade: Abortion and Gender Relations in an Eighteenth-Century New England Village." *William and Mary Quarterly* 48 (1991): 19–49.

Dienes, C. Thomas. *Law, Politics, and Birth Control.* Urbana: University of Illinois Press, 1972.

Himes, Norman E. *Medical History of Contraception.* New York: Gamut Press, 1963.

Mohr, James C. *Abortion in America: The Origins and Evolution of National Policy, 1800–1900.* Oxford: Oxford University Press, 1978.

Reagan, Leslie J. *When Abortion Was a Crime: Women, Medicine, and Law in the United States, 1867–1973.* Berkeley: University of California Press, 1997.

Riegel, Robert E. "The American Father of Birth Control," *New England Quarterly* 6 (1933): 470–90.

Smith-Rosenberg, Carroll. "The Abortion Movement." In *Disorderly Conduct: Visions of Gender in Victorian America.* New York: Alfred A. Knopf, 1985. 217–44.

Tone, Andrea. *Devices and Desires: A History of Contraceptives in America.* New York: Hill and Wang, 2001.

GENDER RELATIONS AND SEXUALITY

Bulloch, Vern L., and Martha Voght. "Homosexuality and Its Confusion with the 'Secret Sin' in Pre-Freudian America." *Journal of the History of Medicine and Allied Sciences* 28 (April 1973): 143–55.

Chauncey, George. *Gay New York: Gender, Urban Culture, and the Making of the Gay Male World, 1890–1940.* New York: Basic Books, 1994.

Chudacoff, Howard P. *The Age of the Bachelor: Creating an American Subculture.* Princeton, N.J.: Princeton University Press, 1999.

Cott, Nancy F. *Public Vows: A History of Marriage and the Nation.* Cambridge, Mass.: Harvard University Press, 2000.

Degler, Carl. "What Ought to Be and What Was: Women's Sexuality in the Nineteenth Century." *American Historical Review* 79 (1974): 1467–90.

Godbeer, Richard. *Sexual Revolution in Early America.* Baltimore: Johns Hopkins University Press, 2002.

Gorn, Elliott J. *The Manly Art: Bare-Knuckle Prize Fighting in America.* Ithaca, N.Y.: Cornell University Press, 1986.

Kern, Louis J. *An Ordered Love: Sex Roles and Sexuality in Victorian Utopias—The Shakers, the Mormons, and the Oneida Community.* Chapel Hill: University of North Carolina Press, 1981.

Laqueur, Thomas W. *Making Sex: Body and Gender from the Greeks to Freud.* Cambridge, Mass.: Harvard University Press, 1990.

Lystra, Karen. *Searching the Heart: Women, Men, and Romantic Love in Nineteenth-Century America.* New York: Oxford University Press, 1989.

Sánchez-Eppler, Karen. *Touching Liberty: Abolition, Feminism, and the Politics of the Body.* Berkeley: University of California Press, 1993.

Sears, Hal D. *The Sex Radicals: Free Love in High Victorian America.* Lawrence: University Press of Kansas, 1977.

Spurlock, John C. *Marriage and Middle-Class Radicalism in America, 1825–1860.* New York: New York University Press, 1988.

Stoehr, Taylor. *Free Love in America: A Documentary History.* New York: AMS Press, 1979.

Talley, Colin L. "Gender and Male Same-Sex Behavior in British North America in the Seventeenth Century." *Journal of the History of Sexuality* 6 (1996): 385–408.

Wagner, Peter. *Eros Revived: Erotica of the Enlightenment in England and America.* London: Secker & Warburg, 1988.

Walters, Ronald G. "The Erotic South: Civilization and Sexuality in American Abolitionism." *American Quarterly* 25 (1973): 177–201.

HEALTH AND MEDICINE

Beall, Otho T., Jr. "Aristotle's Master Piece in America: A Landmark in the Folklore of Medicine." *William and Mary Quarterly* 20 (1963): 207–22.

Cayleff, Susan E. *Wash and Be Healed: The Water-Cure Movement and Women's Health.* Philadelphia: Temple University Press, 1987.

Haller, John S., Jr. *American Medicine in Transition, 1840–1910*. Urbana: University of Illinois Press, 1981.

————. *Medical Protestants: The Eclectics in American Medicine, 1825–1939*. Carbondale: Southern Illinois University Press, 1994.

————, and Robin M. Haller. *The Physician and Sexuality in Victorian America*. Urbana: University of Illinois Press, 1974.

Kett, Joseph K. *The Formation of the American Medical Profession: The Role of Institutions, 1780–1860*. New Haven, Conn.: Yale University Press, 1968.

More, Ellen S. *Restoring the Balance: Women Physicians and the Profession of Medicine, 1850–1995*. Cambridge, Mass.: Harvard University Press, 1999.

Nissenbaum, Stephen. *Sex, Diet, and Debility in Jacksonian America: Sylvester Graham and Health Reform*. Westport, Conn.: Greenwood Press, 1980.

Porter, Roy. " 'The Secrets of Generation Display'd': *Aristotle's Master-piece* in Eighteenth-Century England." *Eighteenth Century Life* 9 (1984–85): 1–16.

Stern, Madeleine B. *Heads and Headlines: The Phrenological Fowlers*. Norman: University of Oklahoma Press, 1971.

Warner, John Harley. *The Therapeutic Perspective: Medical Practice, Knowledge, and Identity in America, 1820–1885*. Cambridge, Mass. Harvard University Press, 1986.

MASTURBATION

Engelhardt, H. Tristram, Jr. "The Disease of Masturbation: Values and the Concept of Disease." *Bulletin of the History of Medicine* 48 (1974): 234–48.

Hunt, Alan. "The Great Masturbation Panic and the Discourses of Moral Regulation in Nineteenth- and Early Twentieth-Century Britain." *Journal of the History of Sexuality* 8 (1998): 575–615.

Laqueur, Thomas W. *Solitary Sex: A Cultural History of Masturbation*. New York: Zone Books, 2003.

Stevenson, David. "Recording the Unspeakable: Masturbation in the Diary of William Drummond, 1657–1659." *Journal of the History of Sexuality* 9 (July 2000): 223–39.

Stolberg, Michael. "Self-pollution, Moral Reform, and the Venereal Trade: Notes on the Sources and Historical Context of *Onania* (1716)." *Journal of the History of Sexuality* 9 (January/April 2000): 37–61.

OBSCENITY, CENSORSHIP, AND PRINT

Ernst, Morris L., and Alan U. Schwartz. *Censorship: The Search for the Obscene*. New York: Macmillan, 1964.

Gertzman, Jay A. *Bookleggers and Smuthounds: The Trade in Erotica, 1920–40*. Philadelphia: University of Pennsylvania Press, 1999.

Gurstein, Rochelle. *The Repeal of Reticence: A History of America's Cultural and Legal Struggles over Free Speech, Obscenity, Sexual Liberation, and Modern Art.* New York: Hill and Wang, 1996.

Hunt, Lynn. "Obscenity and the Origins of Modernity." In *The Invention of Pornography: Obscenity and the Origins of Modernity, 1500–1800,* edited by Lynn Hunt, New York: Zone Books, 1993. 9–45.

Hunter, Ian, David Saunders, and Dugald Williamson. *On Pornography: Literature, Sexuality and Obscenity Law.* New York: St. Martin's Press, 1993.

Kendrick, Walter. *The Secret Museum: Pornography in Modern Culture.* New York: Viking, 1987.

Levy, Leonard W. *Blasphemy: Verbal Defenses against the Sacred, from Moses to Salman Rushdie.* New York: Alfred A. Knopf, 1993.

Marsh, Joss. *Word Crimes: Blasphemy, Culture and Literature in Nineteenth-Century England.* Chicago: University of Chicago Press, 1998.

Paul, James C. N., and Murray L. Schwartz. *Federal Censorship: Obscenity in the Mail.* New York: The Free Press of Glencoe, 1961.

Rabban, David. *Free Speech in Its Forgotten Years.* Cambridge, U.K.: Cambridge University Press, 1997.

Schiller, Dan. *Objectivity and the News: The Public and the Rise of Commercial Journalism.* Philadelphia: University of Pennsylvania Press, 1981.

Scott, George Ryley. *Into Whose Hands: An Examination of Obscene Libel in Its Legal, Sociological and Literary Aspects.* London: Gerald G. Swan, 1945.

Stern, Madeleine B. *Books and Book People in Nineteenth-Century America.* New York: R. R. Bowker Company, 1978.

Thompson, George. *Venus in Boston and Other Tales of Nineteenth-Century City Life.* Edited with an introduction by David S. Reynolds and Kimberly R. Gladman. Amherst: University of Massachusetts Press, 2002.

Thompson, Roger. *Unfit for Modest Ears.* Totowa, N.J.: Rowman and Littlefield, 1979.

Tucher, Andie. *Froth and Scum: Truth, Beauty, Goodness, and the Ax Murder in America's First Mass Medium.* Chapel Hill: University of North Carolina Press, 1994.

RELIGION, REFORM, AND UTOPIANISM

Abzug, Robert H. *Cosmos Crumbling: American Reform and the Religious Imagination.* New York: Oxford University Press, 1994.

Butler, Jon. *Awash in a Sea of Faith: Christianizing the American People.* Cambridge, Mass.: Harvard University Press, 1990.

Eckhardt, Celia Morris. *Fanny Wright, Rebel in America.* Cambridge, Mass.: Harvard University Press, 1984.

Guarneri, Carl J. *The Utopian Alternative: Fourierism in Nineteenth-Century America.* Ithaca, N.Y.: Cornell University Press, 1991.

Leopold, Richard William. *Robert Dale Owen: A Biography.* Cambridge, Mass.: Harvard University Press, 1940.

Rosenberg, Charles E. "The Therapeutic Revolution: Medicine, Meaning, and Social Change in Nineteenth-Century America." *Perspectives in Biology and Medicine* 20 (1977): 485–506.

Silver-Isenstadt, Jean L. *Shameless: The Visionary Life of Mary Gove Nichols.* Baltimore: Johns Hopkins University Press, 2002.

Smith-Rosenberg, Carroll. *Religion and the Rise of the American City: The New York City Mission Movement, 1812–1870.* Ithaca, N.Y.: Cornell University Press, 1971.

Stern, Madeleine B. *The Pantarch: A Biography of Stephen Pearl Andrews.* Austin: University of Texas Press, 1968.

Index

abortion, 23, 26, 42*n*4, 93, 112
　advertisements for, 23, 124–25
　Comstock Law and, 157
　health risks to women, 109, 151
Ackerman, George, 29, 154, 155
adolescent boys. *See also* boys; men;
　　young men
　masturbation and, 72–74
adolescent girls. *See also* girls; women
　employment of, 4
adultery
　masturbation as, 83
　of the mind, 71
advertisements
　for abortion services, 124–25
　for erotic literature, 142–43, 155–56
African Americans
　free, 2
　interracial sexual intercourse, 12, 15,
　　22, 26, 48
　slaves, 2–3
　subordinate status of, 12
alcohol, 14
Alcott, Amos Bronson, 88
Alcott, Louisa May, 88
Alcott, William Andrus, 18, 19
　Physiology of Marriage, The, 88–93
amativeness/organ of, 19, 20*f,* 77, 94,
　　95–97
　denial of, 101–2
　fulfillment of, 114
　in men, 97
　perversion of, 96–98
　unnatural manifestations of, 118
　in women, 97
American Revolution, women and, 3
American Tract Society, 24, 126
animal magnetism, seduction of women
　　and, 146–47

animal nerves, 66, 67–68
appetite, 15, 62–63
Ariel, 134*n*14
Aristotle, 5–6, 7
Aristotle's Master-piece, 5–6, 15, 19, 29
　excerpts, 35–42
　frontispiece, 7*f*
　atheism, fear of, 46–47

bandruche, 64. *See also* condoms
bashfulness, masturbation and, 81
bawdy humor, 6
Beecher, Catharine, 43
Beecher, Henry Ward, 43
Beecher, Lyman, 6, 8
　Perils of Atheism to the Nation, The,
　　46–47
　*Reformation of Morals Practicable and
　　Indispensable, A,* 43–45
　*Resources of the Adversary and Means
　　of Their Destruction,* 45–46
Bell, Luther V., 16, 29
　*Hour's Conference with Fathers and
　　Sons, An,* 74–82
Bennett, James Gordon, 140*n*20
bestiality, 118
Bible
　moral education and, 44, 45
　as obscene, 139, 141
birth control. *See* contraception
birthrate, decline in, 13
blood, as source of sexual desire, 35
Boston Medical and Surgical Journal,
　86
boys. *See also* adolescent boys; young
　　men
　changes in puberty, 113
　masturbation by, 73, 80–81
　seduction of, by prostitutes, 127, 129